Star Wars

Scene-by-Scene

Star Wars
Scene-by-Scene

John David Ebert

ISBN: 1514680572
ISBN-13: 978-1514680575

Acknowledgements

Special thanks go to Michael Aaron Kamins for reading this book in manuscript; JD Casten for his usual expertise; Lawrence Pearce for his incredible cover art; and to my brother Tom Ebert, for his cover design.

Cover artwork:
"Masks and Denatures" by Lawrence Pearce (2015)

Contents

SECOND HALF:
AGAINST THE DEATH STAR   **101**

Introduction:
On *Star Wars* as the
American National Epic

The way I see it, there are three candidates for what would qualify as the American national epic: *Jaws, Star Wars* and *Apocalypse Now*. All three were made around the same time, between 1975 and 1979, and all three are works of celluloid art. So the question then becomes: why should the American national epic be a work of celluloid, rather than literary, genius? Especially when all the great epics of the past, almost without exception, are works of literature. (However, one cannot escape media studies biases even here, since many of these ancient epics, such as *The Iliad* and *The Odyssey*, were originally *sung*, rather than *written*, and were therefore composed in oral rather than literary media).

All the great nations of the past, after all, had *their* great epics. The Indians had, not one but *two* national epics—like the Greeks—an epic of India's dynasty of lunar kings entitled *The Mahabharata*, and one for its solar kings, entitled *The Ramayana*. The Persians had a single mighty epic, literary in nature—whereas the Hindu epics, like those of the Greeks, were originally sung—entitled *The Shahnameh*, composed and written by one Firdausi in the language of Farsi around the year 1000 AD. The Byzantine civilization had a small national epic entitled *Digenis Akritas*, whereas the Georgian national epic was an interesting Medieval tale known as *The Knight in the Panther's Skin* (c. 1200 AD). The honor of having the *oldest* national epic belongs, of course, to the Babylonians, who created *The Epic of Gilgamesh*, whereas the Egyptians really had no national epic at all, or rather, like the Americans—as I'm going to argue in a moment—had one, but in a different medium, for their Books of the Netherworld collectively constituted a kind of national epic, never finished, of the evolution of their conception of the afterlife.

When I was a sophomore English major in college at Arizona State University in the 1980s, professors would pose this question to the class with a certain media studies naivete: what did *we* think the American national epic was, since there didn't seem to be any clear and undisputed candidate? *Moby Dick*? *Huckleberry Finn*? (naïve, that is, in their assumption that such a work, because it had always been of a literary nature in the past, must be in essence of a literary nature *today* to count as a national epic). After all, each of the Western nations seemed to have produced clear literary epics of what is known as a secondary, or "written" nature (primary epics being those which were originally oral in nature and then written down later). England had produced Milton's *Paradise Lost*; Italy had Dante's *Divine Comedy*; Spain had *The Cid*; France had *The Song of Roland*; and Germany had Wagner's great operatic *Der Ring des Nibelungen* (but in this case, take note, in a medium that was *other than* merely literary). Why not an American national epic, then, that was equivalent in nature to these and which celebrated American values?

The problem was—and still is, however—that it has never been very clear precisely what those values *are*, because they differ from region to region, depending upon whom you ask, as Joel Garreau figured out in his book on *The Nine Nations of North America*.[1] The values of the North, for instance, are traditionally industrial, whereas those of the South have been agrarian. (Hence, *Moby Dick* as a northern epic, an epic of hunters and dollar trappers; whereas *Huckleberry Finn* qualifies as a southern epic, a riverrine epic, furthermore, that celebrates the long, slow exploration of the American pastoral landscape).

Out West, things get even more problematic, for there seems to be no national epic at all unless one points to works of kitschy science fiction like *Dune* as the national epic of Southern California, or *Neuromancer* as the national epic of Silicon Valley in the north. And if we were to uphold, for the Midwest, Longfellow's *Song of Hiawatha*, one feels like this might be an example of cheating, since it is a form of colonialization of another people's myths and cannot by definition be held up as representing specifically *American* values, since the values of the myths discussed by Longfellow belong to another people that were here *before* the whites settled and conquered with genocidal violence the plains of the Midwest.

Stephen King's bizarre multi-volume *Dark Tower* epic would seem to be a candidate just by virtue of its length, but it is far too full of goofy kitsch and syrupy sentimentality to qualify, with dignity, as something that one could hold up as a repository of national values.

So the problem, when it comes to establishing grounds for an American epic, seems to be that as far as its written literature is concerned, the values expressed are inevitably far too regional for the work in question to represent anything as vast and all-encompassing as a work embodying "national values."

For that, we must turn to the cinema, a *very* American popular art form which, however, was transformed in the 1970s from a mere collection of kitsch and melodramatic genres—i.e. thrillers, Westerns and spy movies--to something much closer to a literary art form, for the cinema of the 1970s was the American response to the European avant-garde New Wave of cinema that appeared immediately after the war. The highbrow cultural sensibilities represented by such films as Truffaut's *Jules and Jim*; or Fellini's *La Dolce Vita*; or Antonioni's *L'Avventura*; or Godard's *Breathless* were massively influential on that generation of American directors known as The Film School Generation, which emerged out of the collapsing *ancien regime* of the Hollywood studio system of the 1960s. The sensibilities of filmmakers like Peter Bogdanovich with his adaptation of Larry McMurtry's novel *The Last Picture Show*; or Martin Scorsese's *Taxi Driver* (with its screenplay penned by the *very* literate Paul Schrader); or Francis Ford Coppola's *Godfather* films; or Roman Polanski's *Chinatown* (with its cultured screenwriter, Robert Towne); all of this was, quite simply, something never seen in Hollywood before. (And here, the Modernists' experience of screenwriting in Hollywood back in the 1930s and 40s doesn't count as a precedent, because the efforts of writers like Nathanael West, William Faulkner, Ernest Hemingway or Raymond Chandler were nearly always bowdlerized and ended up turning these men into angry, bitter alcoholics frustrated by the Hollywood megamachine and its almighty studio producers, who held *all* the power in those days).

So, with the shift in power to the directors themselves—Robert Altman, Stanley Kubrick, Hal Ashby, Brian De Palma et. al.--the values of 1970s film were becoming more and more literary, shaping Hollywood cinema into a "respectable" art form at last, one "respectable" enough at least to sit alongside the same shelf with the achievements of the European avant-garde.

Which brings us back to our consideration of *Jaws, Apocalypse Now* and *Star Wars*—films which came out of this milieu and which made their very existence possible in the first place--as the only three possible candidates for a national American epic. The problem with *Apocalypse Now*, however, in assuming that particular laurel wreath, is that its values are almost *exclusively* literary. These films were coming along, after all, at the tail end of the age of McLuhan's *Understanding Media* (1964)[2] in which he created an American theoretical milieu—admittedly from Toronto—that understood *all* media from the point of view of literary values (McLuhan thought, for instance, that Madison Avenue advertising was *the* great art form of the age).[3] So *Apocalypse Now*, though it retrieves the epic as a genre, is simply *too* literary, in an old-fashioned sense, to exemplify the multi-mediatic nature of the zeitgeist of that time.

The problem with *Jaws*, on the other hand, though it reterritorializes Melville's *Moby Dick* for a mass audience, is that it is not literary enough. It is *strictly* mass entertainment, though its values are inherently American (hunting the white whale as the ultimate dollar hunt becomes hunting the Great White Shark as the American patriarchal family hero's means of protecting his suburban family and keeping them safe from What's Out There). And besides, as far as genres go—and in spite of its grand heroic gestures--*Jaws* feels more like a thriller than an epic.

Star Wars, however, when it came out in 1977, was a work of pop art that engulfed absolutely *all* previous media. Its values were not strictly—or even primarily--literary, of course, but then this was no longer a strictly literary age, as McLuhan in his works had made clear. New York had already, a decade or so earlier, redefined "Pop Art" as a form of high art in disguise with Andy Warhol's Brillo Boxes and Roy Lichtenstein's comic book panel blow-ups. So the boundaries between "highbrow" and "lowbrow" art were no longer so clear by the time 1977 rolled around (the graffiti art of Jean-Michel Basquiat lay just around the corner as Pop Art's grand finale during the 1980s).

Star Wars functioned as a kind of cultural midden heap which simply dumped *all* previous media into its containing frames and hybridized them into an entire cosmos of dead space junk and old, rusty used-up worlds borrowed from science fiction novels like *Dune* and *Foundation*; 1930s comic strips like *Flash Gordon*[4] and 1960s comic books like *The Fantastic Four*;[5] images and indeed, whole scenes, were taken from Westerns, World War II movies, Kurosawa's samurai films, and noir classics like *The Maltese Falcon*. It was truly a multi-media epic for an age of "Understanding" the literary potential inherent in *all* media. (In French theory across the water, meanwhile, Roland Barthes with his *Mythologies*[6] and the early books of Jean Baudrillard[7] were performing a function equivalent to what McLuhan was doing in Toronto). If it is true that, as McLuhan always said, every new medium proceeds by swallowing up a previous medium, then *Star Wars* engulfed *all* media in just the same way that YouTube, for instance, engulfs all previous *electronic* media.

Furthermore—and perhaps even more importantly— *Star Wars* evades the problem of American regionalism faced by previous literary epics through transforming its examination of American values into "spheres" and "orbs" that are region-free and non-specific. The Death Star is a sphere that represents the post-war American Empire that is still in the process of effacing and erasing the local and overcoding it into the world interior of capital, as Peter Sloterdijk put it in his book *In the World Interior of Capital*.[8] And just as Sloterdijk held up the Crystal Palace of the London Exhibition of 1851 as *the* primary metaphor for today's global world of endless consumption, so Lucas's Death Star performs a similar function of "destroying worlds" by erasing their local codes and recoding them into the value neutral and gray colors of the Empire which homogenizes everything it comes near.

Tatooine is the movie's other great sphere of values: it is a waste land of economic traps and prisons, but one that must be tamed by the particularly American values of the West: rugged individualism, cowboy shoot-outs and Midwestern farmer's values. The Death Star, by contrast, is industrial and, on the face of it, Northern in essence, but since the North's values have overcoded the entire continent—not to mention the whole of the green and blue globe of the earth—it too manages to evade the fate of regionalism.

So *Star Wars* is a Tale of Two Orbs, for the friction between Tatooine and the Death Star—and I have framed my analysis in this book in two halves based on this polarity--is the difference engine that drives the narrative forward. There are two other orbs, Alderaan (which we never find out anything about) and the rebel base on the moon of Yavin, which is a forest planet that simply refers to the Ecotopic values of Northern California. So, Tatooine for the West—and recall that Lucas even borrows an entire scene from John Ford's *The Searchers*—and the forest moon of Yavin for California, while the Death Star upholds the originally industrial values of the now decaying rust belt of the North and East Coast. *Star Wars*, that is to say, engulfs *everything*, including even the regional values that have, thus far, prevented American literary theoreticians from holding a consensus on the American national epic.

The film, furthermore, has all the necessary characteristics that would qualify it as a descendant of the ancient traditional oral and literary epics: it begins in what is called *medias res* (i.e. "in the middle of things") with Episode 4, as though the viewer had just inadvertently walked into the middle of an already ongoing narrative; it features huge battles between contending armies struggling for possession of the cosmos, as in Milton's *Paradise Lost* with its battle between the armies of the rebel angels and the heavenly hierarchies, or *The Mahabharata*, with its eighteen volume long epic struggle for control over north India by two families, the Kauravas and the Pandavas, who are related by blood. The values of *Star Wars* are, as I have said, also nationalistic, and like Virgil's *The Aeneid*, they advertise—if they don't exactly advocate—the values of Empire as a problem still to be solved.

Star Trek, on the other hand—which some have (perhaps half-jokingly) put forward as an example of the great American epic--simply doesn't fit the bill: it is a *series*, not an epic, and its concerns are not the traditional epic ones of struggle for power over a cosmos by two mighty contending armies, but rather a nerdy group of space explorers who find new things and new enemies to grapple with in each episode. It is a vehicle with which to explore the implications of the scientific-industrial complex, but its concerns are confined *strictly* to that context. Also, the episodes themselves are generally self-contained and have no necessary relation to each other, as they *must* in a properly functioning epic. Indeed, *Star Trek* has *no* qualities of a national epic, whereas *Star Wars* has *all* of them.

Star Wars, then, *is* the Great American National Epic,

and in the age of multimedia, being a work of literature is simply no longer one of the conditions necessary to fulfill this role. In theory, an epic could've emerged from *any* of the new media that have come along since World War II: television, graphic novels, the Internet, etc. But it came out of Hollywood cinema because the environmental conditions—as they were in the earth's pre-biotic epoch, in which the chemical conditions for the emergence of living cells happened once and was never again repeated—were just right.

And we, as Americans, are just as proud of it as the Germans were when Wagner forged a national epic for *them*, not out of a work of literature exactly, but out of the musical genre of opera.

So, let us begin the exploration of the first volume—as it were—in the installment of the great and, significantly, ongoing—don't forget that *The Mahabharata* went on for eighteen volumes and is simply too long to read unabridged by any Westerner—saga of the clash between imperial globalization and local regionalism; between ecotopic systems theorists and multi-billionaire capitalists; between rugged individualists and liberal collectives; between anarchists who "want government out" of their business, and the techno-fascism of ever more and more new technologies of discipline and control to keep us ever more and more tightly under control.

Yes, it's all in there: everything that is going on across this planet right now, today, nearly 30 years after the release of that first film. Its themes are *still* current, and *still* pertinent to our contemporary situation.

It is, after all, an epic...

...PROPOSITION 2. The angles formed by the planets, e.g. right angles, squares, oppositions, etc. are masculine and are contained on the *inside* of the zodiac, which functions as a uteromorphic container within which they are inscribed. They are on the *inside* of the mother's body. But with the surrounding of the earth by satellites, this order was reversed and the round sphere of the earth was encompassed and surrounded by the masculine technologies born through the paternal womb of the Metaphysical Age (think here, not only of Athena, but of the Christ-being, incarnate as the Logos, uttered as the Word from the Father's mouth [the Metaphysical Age begins not with Plato, as Heidegger insisted, but rather with Moses and Homer])...

...PROPOSITION 4. The city did not become truly "uteromorphic" until it attained the status of a modern sphere. A sphere is a uterine container. The cities of the ancient world, despite the insistences of Lewis Mumford and Peter Sloterdijk to the contrary, were not truly uteromorphic, since they were not actually coterminous with the globe of the earth itself. An ancient city or polis surrounded by a wall is actually *exoskeletal* in nature rather than uteromorphic, strictly speaking. (They rarely occur in the form of perfect circles, although ancient cities like Mari and Baghdad were circular in shape). Most ancient cities had protective outer shells in the form of walls encasing the soft pink anatomies inside them.

Corollary. Those characters in *Star Wars* which can be termed "exoskeletal," i.e. wear outer shells to encase their inner anatomies, are always given a negative valency (i.e. they are on the Dark Side). They are like the early prehistoric fish known as Placoderms, which at first had bony outer shells that gradually vanished over time in favor of the speed and mobility given to them without the shell casings. Characters, then, such as Darth Vader, Boba Fett or the stormtroopers are "Placodermic" in nature. Those characters opposing them never wear bony outer shells. They are exposed and vulnerable, and they signify a "mammalian" evolutionary advance over the Placoderms and reptiles (for instance, stormtroopers riding on giant lizards, etc.).

--fragment taken from "The Elements of Star Wars" *(see Appendix)*

FIRST HALF:
THE ESCAPE FROM TATOOINE

The Opening Crawl:
"Episode IV: A New Hope"9
(0:00 – 1:42)

Whereas *Apocalypse Now* had begun without a title sequence, *Star Wars* begins with an explosive title that erupts at the viewer and rapidly recedes into outer space, while a floating inscription crawls forward in triangular shape into the receding distance, as though it were laid out on a flat plane thrusting into three-dimensional, perspectival space. The crawl provides the film's opening synopsis, like the synopses at the start of each chapter of Milton's *Paradise Lost*, which inform the reader, in summary fashion, of the events of that chapter. The crawl recedes into the depths of space in a fashion that reiterates the discovery of the laws of depth perspective in the Renaissance art of the fifteenth century. It is a capturing and retrieval of the entire optical world and its theories—derived from Al-Hazen's treatise on optics—of the discovery of three-dimensional space in the Renaissance.

So we have begun with an homage to Euclid's *Elements* as *the* foundational text (first translated into Latin in 1120 AD) of the mathematics that made possible the entirety of the mechanized society which we currently take for granted today, while Al-Hazen's *Kitab al-Manazir* (or, *The Book of Optics*)—from whence the optical theories were derived that eventually led to the creation of the camera and so to the entire world of cinematic spectacle—was translated from Arabic into Latin near the end of the twelfth century.

The Mechanization of Civilization, which it has been the planetary task of the West to achieve, was thus made possible by optical theories about seeing things spread out in space as a single overall container. Every entity, in such a space, is scaled to the same dimensions. Pharaoh, the Virgin Mary, or Christ Pantocrator no longer tower over all the other figures who are diminished to insignificance on Byzantine mosaics and the walls of churches. In perspectival space, all entities are scaled to the same dimension and no importance is given to any single one of them in preference to the others. In other words, *it is the space itself* which has taken on a spiritual importance in Renaissance art, rather than particular iconic entities.

The inceptual paragraph of the crawl informs us that we are entering into the midst of a gigantic civil war in which rebel troops fighting a Galactic Empire have found a hidden secret base (on a jungle planet, as it turns out, like the Vietcong hiding in the jungles away from the ever-vigilant eyes of the American Empire during the Vietnam War).

The second paragraph of the crawl informs us that these rebels have managed to steal the plans for the Empire's ultimate weapon, known as the Death Star, an armored space station with the power to destroy entire planets. The Death Star, as it turns out, is an exoskeletal imitation of a planet. More specifically, it is a metaphor for the circumnavigated and globally-citified earth ("the urb it orbs," as Joyce put it in *Finnegans Wake*),[10] surrounded with satellites that have had the effect of putting the uteromorphic[11] sphere of the mother's body on the *inside* of the angular weapons of the masculine mentality (the exact *inverse* of an astrological natal chart, let's say, where the planetary geometries formed by the angles are surrounded by the zodiac). The earth is very much today—and has been since 1957--like an armored space station with nuclear missiles potentially powerful enough to destroy asteroids, moons and possibly even other planets. It has *become* a Death Star. So, note that the mother's body has already been captured and surrounded by the mechanizations of the mindborn children of the paternal womb.

In the third paragraph, we are told that Princess Leia is travelling aboard a tiny ship with the stolen plans for the Death Star which will reveal the Achilles Heel of the space station, by means of which the guerilla force of the rebel army might possibly destroy it. Princess Leia, as we will see shortly, is the Earth Mother herself, corresponding to Wagner's Erda, who rises up out of the ground in his opera *Die Gotterdammerung* to pronounce the Fate of all the gods and heroes of the Norse pantheon.

The Capture of Princess Leia
(1:42 – 8:48)

The camera now pans down to reveal a pair of bluish-gray moons hovering over the tan-and-copper surface of the planet Tatooine, while a tiny ship, whose posterior end is composed mainly of a series of three rows of circles propelling it forward, seeks to evade the laser blasts of a gigantic ship that now comes into view from the top of the screen (a visual quotation from the shot of the "endless" spaceship *Discovery* on its way to Jupiter in *2001: A Space Odyssey*). The pursuing ship, known as an Imperial Star Destroyer, is colossal, and its immensity as it engulfs the screen is designed to overawe the viewer with a sense of its all-encompassing military power. *No* signifiers can escape the reach of its planetary grasp, as though it were coming to enclose the planet below inside of an enormous exoskeleton. The ship is in the form of a gigantic arrow-head, and it swoops down to engulf the tiny fleeing rebel ship, sucking it up inside the fluorescent-lit bay of its interior.

Inside the rebel ship, meanwhile, which is composed entirely of hallways and corridors of brightly lit white paneling, C3P0 and R2D2 are in a state of disoriented panic as they scramble about the hallways looking for a means of egress.

The main hatchway to the rebel ship is then blasted open from the other side by stormtroopers wearing white exoskeletal suits, while a tall black figure, also wearing an exoskeleton—black in his case—steps through the opening as rebel soldiers (wearing only helmets, but otherwise garbed in clothing) run down the hallways from the pursuing stormtroopers.

Princess Leia, her hair designed in Hopi-headdress fashion as two large circles on either side of her head, and wearing a thin white dress, steps forth out of the dark bluish-red shadows to slide a disc into R2D2's memory banks (the disc contains the plans for the Death Star as well as a holographic message of distress for Obi-Wan Kenobi). She sends R2 on his way and then waits in the shadowy corridor, gun in hand, as a cluster of stormtroopers enters the engine room, spots her and shoots her down with a bluish-white stun circle. They carry her away as a prisoner for Darth Vader.

The droids, meanwhile, C3P0 and R2D2, clamber into an escape pod, while a confused C3P0 asks his partner just what type of plans he's going on about. He nevertheless follows R2 into the pod, for he has little choice, and the pod drops away from the rebel ship with a blast of breaking bolts and clamps that unleash it from the ship's white metallic mother body.

Now, just as the giant Star Destroyer had come down from above to engulf the tiny rebel ship, the escape pod drops with gravitational force *downwards* toward the pull of the huge desert planet below.

The young princess, meanwhile, is brought before Darth Vader, who points an accusing finger at her and demands to

32

know where the plans for the Death Star have been hidden. Leia insists she knows nothing of any such plans and that she was merely on a diplomatic mission to Alderaan. Vader scoffs at this, which he knows is a lie, and tells his men to take her away.

He grabs one rebel by the neck and lifts him into the air with apparent superhuman strength, demanding to know the location of the plans, but the man insists that he doesn't know either and Vader, disgusted, tosses him to the ground. When one of his administrative officials tells him that a pod with no life forms aboard recently jettisoned toward the planet below, Vader's intuition tells him—correctly, as it turns out—that the plans have been hidden in the pod and he orders a detachment to be sent down to the planet to retrieve the pod.

Hence, the arrowhead-shaped star destroyer captures a rebel ship that is associated with tiny circles, and imprisons a princess with symmetrical circles in her hair. Masculine angularity, in other words, has captured and engulfed the domain of the Mother, whose contours are always curvilinear. The princess is, as I have said, Wagner's Erda, the Earth Mother herself, who has been overcoded by the semiotics of Father Science. Leia's capture reiterates in miniature the engulfing of the earth by the institutions of Big Science. She is placed *inside* the Death Star, a metaphor for the exoskeletal armoring of technics that has surrounded the earth itself and swallowed it up with the machines and grid-lines born from the womb of Father Science during the Metaphysical Age.

In astrology, the Tenth House is associated with the paternal order—equivalent to Lacan's Name of the Father— while its opposing house, the Fourth, is the house of the Mother, that is to say, all *Abgrund*-source energies.[12] It is the capturing of Mother Right, in other words, by Father Right, which has, as Heidegger put it, "enframed" the earth with technological codes that have the effect of de-worlding into the mode of *Vorhandenheit* any entities which it encounters.[13] *Vorhandenheit* refers to the realm of self-sufficient entities in Heideggerian discourse: it is the grid that captures and locks them into Cartesian phase space, with their x, y, z coordinates translating all their concrete, sensory values into mathematical vectors that are strictly *quantitative*, rather than *qualitative*. All entities captured into this grid can be charted and mapped, pulled apart and recoded, but they will be *de-worlded* entities torn from the structural couplings with their ecological environments, like the dinosaurs in *Jurassic Park*. It is precisely the phase space, however, that is necessary for the creation and generation of machines, which must be visualized in such a three dimensional space in order to create complex mechanical devices, rather than the merely simple wind and water-driven machines of what Lewis Mumford once termed the Eotechnic era: an age in which technology did not stand out but was embedded in the environment and powered by the natural forces of wind, water, and wood.[14] During the Paleotechnic, however, which coincides with the advent of Cartesian phase space, machines stepped into the foreground and were born from out of the paternal womb—the grid, that is to say, of three-dimensional phase space—that is characteristic of translating and recoding entities into the mode of *Vorhandenheit*.

But what happens when *all* entities have been captured and recoded by the sign regime of the phase space of Father Right? The capturing of Princess Leia, who is essentially the "anima" of the earth itself, is tantamount to the enframing of the planet by the value-neutral and nihilistic grid of these scientistic forces, the forces, in particular, of the kinds of J. Robert Oppenheimer Big Science institutions that came into being after World War II.

That is what the Empire in *Star Wars* signifies: the world of big business--the corporate hi-jacking of the sciences and the universities and their overcoding[15] by the military-- which has resulted in the contemporary GPS World which we find ourselves inhabiting today.

The Princess, Erda herself, that is to say, *has* been captured and overcoded by Father Right and his technical semiotic sign regime.

In order to liberate her from her prison, a "new hope" will be required, in the form of a young naïf who recovers the lost art of divining the earth's etheric energy forces which the merely quantitative grids of science have paved over.

To put it in the language of astrology, the Tenth House— the order of the Father—has swallowed up the Fourth House—that of the Mother—and requires a figure from the First House with a developed sense of self to liberate her. But that will require taking the Long Journey of the Ninth House (which is known as the House of Long Journeys, i.e. speculative cosmological and theological problems) in order to meet the Father in the Tenth House on his own ground.[16]

But first, a Short Journey—i.e. the Third House, directly opposite the Ninth—will be required through the domestic sphere—the Fourth House—in order to begin moving into the problem-solving of tasks which the Sixth House, the House of Small Animals, represents. R2D2 and C3P0 are precisely the "small animals" that Luke Skywalker will be given as companions in place of the birds and furry companions from the fairy tales of the ancient past, before the earth was recoded by the semiotics of Father Science, who has appropriated all of the creative powers from the Mother and seeks to provide technological substitutes for everything that she is capable of producing naturally. Thus, natural childbirth will be replaced by in vitro fertilization; sexual reproduction will be decoupled, by chemical means of "the pill," from the actual production of offspring; and the grains of the earth will be traded out for the GMO's of big agribusiness corporations like Monsanto.

That is the meaning of the capture of Princess Leia in the opening scenes of George Lucas's *Star Wars*.

The Capture of the Droids

(8:48 – 15:10)

A shot of the Imperial Star Destroyer drifting over the desert planet of Tatooine, laced with silvery-blue striations, then follows, giving the viewer a basic vector: from above *downwards*. These are spirit beings which have fallen to earth and they have escaped from the spiritually masculine order of Father Right.

Down on the ground below, meanwhile, C3PO and R2D2 have made their way out of the escape pod, which has crash-landed onto the crest of a dune. The two characters are always arguing—they have been taken from a similar pair of characters in Kurosawa's *The Hidden Fortress*, as is well known—and the present argument concerns which direction they should go: R2 insists that he is on a *mission*, which C3P0—who is always in the dark about everything—professes to know nothing about. He insists on going to the *right*, whereas R2 heads off on his own in the opposite direction.

They are silver and gold, these two (R2's circular revolving head, at least, is silver, with his black mono-eye borrowed from that of HAL 9000 in *2001: A Space Odyssey*):

that is to say, they are embodiments of cosmic principles, for silver and gold were the metals in alchemy associated with the moon (silver) and the sun (gold), metals which were thought to have actually been woven into the minerals and rocks of the earth by the rotations of those heavenly bodies themselves, moving around it like a spider spinning its web.

C3P0 then heads off across a valley of giant tan-brown sand dunes across which has been splayed the wasted skeleton of some long dead reptilian beast from another age, an age perhaps in which the climate was different and could support the water requirements of such Leviathans.

C3P0 curses his bad luck until he sees something flashing on the horizon: a glint of hope towards which he now begins making his way, although we find out soon enough that he is only running towards his own captivity.

R2D2 fares no better, however, as the next shot displays him in a dark vermilion canyon at twilight, seeming, like a character out of an old Grimm's fairy tale, to have lost his way in a forest. That impression is further heightened by the presence of little desert creatures known as Jawas who are garbed in brown clothing and hide in the niches of the canyon, from whence they peer out, waiting for prey. Only their bright gleaming gold eyes can be seen, reminding the viewer of the motif of the character lost at night in a forest surrounded by the luminous eyes of various strange and terrible creatures.

The Jawas are essentially a transcription into the language of science fiction of Bedouin tribesmen who make their living capturing runaway slaves and taking them to towns and villages to put them up for sale. The droids here are plugged into the semiotic slot of runaway slaves, like Joseph who was rescued from the well his brothers had thrown him into and then sold into slavery. That apparently random course of events, however, led him to his destiny as vizier of Egypt, just as the capture of R2D2 and C3P0, a chance event, sets in motion a chain of circumstances that lands them right at the center of the power struggle of Empire against the Rebellion.

Whereas Princess Leia had been captured by the technological megamachine of Big Science (i.e. corporate-university science coupled with the military state apparatus) the droids replicate the Gnostic myth of the soul's fall, sinking and capture of beings of light, sent from a world "above," who are trapped on the plane of physical materiality.[17] But, just as in Gnosticism, in which the soul is on a mission to eventually recover its memories of a lost world of light and luminosity, the droids, too, are emissaries from a higher world bearing a message of light to the One who is trapped in the domesticity of what in astrology is known as the Fourth House; that, namely, of the sphere of the mother.

The Jawas now send a bolt of electricity hurling at R2D2, which causes him to seize up and topple over. The little tribesmen then scurry about, collecting him and carrying him back toward their gigantic, rusty iron Sandcrawler. In Bedouin days, the droids-as-slaves would have been thrown into the inside of some cart pulled by camels, perhaps, but in the Age of Grand Mechanization, the camels and donkeys have been replaced by internal combustion machines pulled in lumbering fashion by tank treads.

It is no coincidence that slavery existed throughout the entire course of human history only until the time of the Industrial Revolution, when machines were at last mastered enough to replace and do the work previously done by slaves. Slavery, that is, ended only when machines were complex enough to become their replacements and do the work for them. Hence, R2D2 and C3P0 are slaves recoded into the semiotics of a post-industrial age dominated by machines.

The Jawas place a restraining bolt on R2—the equivalent of shackling a slave—and then he is sucked up into the interior of the enormous and ancient Sandcrawler, and once inside, he discovers that he has been tossed into the junk heap of various other renegade robots. The Jawas make their living tracking down sundry escaped robots and putting them back onto the market for resale.

C3P0, his gleaming gold carapace shining in the dim interior of the Sandcrawler, recognizes his pal and is overjoyed to see him. But an uncertain fate has befallen them both and casts a pall of gloom over their reunion.

The droids have been ripped from their function as servants to the Rebels and must now be recoded as commodities to be put up for sale. They are flows, in other words, which, like any flow of the capitalist order—water, electricity, gasoline, etc.—must be stopped, arrested and coded with new flows that send them into circulation on the global market.

Thus, Lucas recodes the Gnostic myth so that the soul's fall and captivity into the world of physical matter—the "soul cages" as the musician Sting, capturing the same myth back in the 1980s, rightly called them—becomes the fall and entry of the soul into the economic order of capital.

But their capture is a necessary one and forms a parallel to Princess Leia's, who represents the Earth principle itself that has been captured and over-gridded by GPS technologies that are state-sponsored, supported and administrated. (Think of the fall and capture of the Tom Hanks character in Steven Spielberg's 1994 film *The Terminal*, who suffers a similar fate). In order to rescue her, the droids must undergo a parallel fall, but in the *opposite* direction, for whereas Leia has been sucked *upwards* into the realm of Spirit, the droids have fallen *downwards* into the realm of Soul. But it is a fall without which Leia cannot be redeemed from her captivity inside the exoskeletal order of the Death Star. (Note that the Jawas are the very opposite of exoskeletal: all we see of them are their glittering eyes which, like Spanish gold doubloons, mirror the mercantile values which they represent, while their bodies are hidden and garbed within the soft folds of their dusty brown robes, for as "Subjects" they are complete anonymities).

42

Introduction of Luke Skywalker

(15:10 – 19:40)

Lucas makes use of an old-fashioned wipe as a transition to the next scene, which in the 1997 re-release of the film with newly added CGI effects shows a detachment of stormtroopers riding on the backs of huge lizard-like beasts (whereas in the original 1977 theatrical release, there was only one stormtrooper mounted atop a miserable frozen sculpture of a lizard in the far background). The 1997 re-release, however, was tantamount to the beginnings of the *end* of the classic period of special effects cinema which Lucas had inaugurated with his "formative" *Star Wars* in 1977, so it is fitting that in the 1997 version, he is preparing to bring that great age to a close as he warms up for his *Star Wars* prequels. Though I admit that the 1997 version of the scene is a considerable improvement over the originally lifeless image, the lizard beasts are not *quite* convincing to the eye; in fact, they look much *less* convincing than the dinosaurs which Spielberg had created using the same kinds of effects only three years earlier with *Jurassic Park*, a film that ended once and for all the Ray Harryhausen[18] era of special effects miniatures and stop motion animation and began the slide of celluloid / analogue cinema toward its downfall into hyper-digitization.

Note, though, that the stormtroopers are beings wearing exoskeletal suits who have come down to earth from the stars, and so it is fitting that they are riding on the backs of lizard beasts, since reptiles are invariably given a chthonic valency in ancient myth, for they are creatures of the sub-lunary realm of the earth. The exoskeletal stormtroopers along with their reptilian beasts, then, are associated with *regressed* and *primordial* zoological creatures. (The biomorphologies of both insects and crustaceans are exoskeletal, whereas reptiles are not, yet they share in common with insects that they all lay eggs. Insects, crustaceans and reptiles, that is, have not yet attained to the warm, pink bodies with mammalian wombs and more highly evolved emotional brains capable of nurturing and caring for their young). The point of the scene semiotically speaking, then, is that there is something cold and reptilian about the Empire and its exoskeletal characters.

In the next scene, the Jawas have stopped their Sandcrawler at a nearby moisture farm, and they force R2D2 and C3P0 to get out along with five or so other droids, which they line up like slaves for sale to the farmer who, in this case, happens to be Uncle Owen and his foster child Luke Skywalker, whom we meet here for the first time. It is of vital importance to note that Luke comes *up* from out of the dome-shaped house—which is actually a sort of tool shed—followed by his uncle. His aunt immediately calls to him, however, from the living area, which is a round pit that has been dug into the earth utilizing various tunnels to create cave-like rooms that have been burrowed into it. Luke peers down over the edge while his Aunt informs him that if his uncle decides to buy a translator robot to be sure that the robot speaks Bocci. Luke tells her that it doesn't look like they have much of a choice but he assures her that he will remind his uncle anyway.

The architecture of Luke's home, then, is composed of two separate units: the domical-shaped tool shed which resembles a miniature mosque; and the pit in the earth where the living quarters are located. Luke, in other words, *has actually emerged from the earth itself*. He and his family are earth-burrowers, like the kinds of desert creatures— meerkats, moles, prairie dogs, etc.—that dig holes into the ground and form their homes out of them. He is therefore tied very strongly with the energies of the earthly element, though his last name, "Skywalker," refers to another, hidden pedigree from the Spirit World up above. He is a being, in other words, with the potential to unite *both* worlds.

In order to rescue the captured Princess Leia, the earth goddess herself, a being from the earth is required as a sort of twin or counterpart to her (just as Ben Kenobi will form the twin and counterpart to Darth Vader, for they are old enemies). Earthly energies will be required to extract her from the prison of the Death Star.

Note, too, that the semiotics of the Empire are global: it is attempting to capture the earth and imprison it inside of a GPS world of satellites, drones and an electromagnetic web that captures, surrounds and encompasses its curvilinearity with masculine, angular thinking. In the present scene, however, we have gone to a very *local* and specific *place* on the earth, from out of which it gives birth to its hero who will fight the globalizing Empire. Like the jihadists hiding in the caves and underground fortresses in the mountains of Afghanistan, they are earthly desert dwellers who have chosen to take on the Empire, a vast system based upon the erasure and nihilism of all localities whatsoever. Every place—the Empire desires—must become like every other: homogenized architecture, airports and shopping malls dominated by big corporations with vast and limitless power. (The Empire in *Star Wars is* Negri and Hardt's Empire which the multitude is busy fighting).[19]

The Jawas line up their droids, most of which have very zoomorphic, crustacean qualities about them. They look like they might have been dredged up from beneath the ocean during its Cambrian explosion of proto-animal forms. (One of them vaguely resembles Robby the Robot from the 1956 film *Forbidden Planet*). *Only* C3P0, however, has anthropomorphic qualities. He is chosen and purchased by Uncle Owen specifically for his *language* abilities and facility in communicating with other machines. He therefore stands out as more "evolved" than they.

Instead of buying R2D2, however, Uncle Owen purchases a red unit that resembles him, but no sooner does it roll forward than it blows a circuit, which infuriates Owen, who begins to haggle with the Jawa merchants. C3P0, meanwhile, advises Luke to tell his uncle to purchase R2D2, with whom he has worked regularly before, and so the uncle agrees to exchange the red unit for R2, or "the blue one," as he refers to him (for he has come down from the sky). R2 then rolls excitedly forward, for his mind is on the mission which Princess Leia programmed him to do: find Obi-Wan Kenobi. If the red droid hadn't broken down at the right moment, R2 would never have been able to deliver the message of light to Kenobi, but Destiny has set things up so that little accidents have big results.

We only ever see one side of the world: that is to say, it shows its visible face to us, a world that is composed out of *apparently* deterministic cause and effect reactions between material bodies. But its spiritual and purposive side is always turned *away* from us, so that we can only ever guess at the intentions which the Transcendent World has for us. And it expresses its intentions and purposes precisely through little accidents and chance events that open up temporal pathways through which specific pre-destined purposes must be fulfilled.

The scene ends with Luke taking the droids with him downward into the tool shed. Note that both the tool shed and the dwelling quarters have circular shapes and are therefore uteromorphic in nature, in accordance with our initial axioms. The angular thinking of the Empire must be fought from the uteromorphic world of the circular and the feminine, and that is precisely where its hero must then be found and retrieved, fished out of an apparently innocuous location in the middle of a desert waste land.

The Discovery of the Message

(19:11 – 22:33)

Inside the tool shed now, C3P0 finds relief in descending into an oil bath while Luke works on cleaning the "carbon scoring" from R2D2. (C3P0's oil bath reiterates the vector of descent of the droids: that, namely, from above *downwards*. They come down from above, whereas he meets them coming up from below. Together, they represent the energies of spirit and matter meeting and crossing to form a sort of etheric Star of David). C3P0 then formally introduces himself and R2D2 so that now both the viewer and Luke know their names.

Luke is just in the middle of trying to fix something that he has found blocking R2's circuits, and he is saying, "Were you on a starcruiser or...?" when a holographic message beams out from R2 like a movie projector, showing an image of a tiny princess begging for help from someone named "Obi-Wan Kenobi." Luke claims that though he doesn't know anyone named "Obi-Wan," he *does* know of a strange old hermit named Ben Kenobi, who lives out beyond the dune sea.

Luke says that he better play back the message and reaches for a different tool, but C3P0 tells him that R2 has just informed him that if he removes his restraining bolt then perhaps the message will play better. When Luke does so, however, the grainy, low-rez image of the princess disappears, and he demands that R2 play it back. R2 insists, however, that it was just some "old data," nothing for Luke to be concerned about.

Luke's aunt then calls him in for lunch, and he hands the tool over to C3P0, telling him to see what he can do. When Luke is gone, C3P0 admonishes his companion to reconsider playing back that message, but R2 ignores him, asking instead if he thinks that Luke likes him at all. When C3P0 tells him that he most likely does not, R2 asks his companion whether, perhaps, *he* likes him? 3P0 then testily informs him that he doesn't really like him either.

Luke is trapped inside what in astrology is known as the Fourth House, that of the domestic sphere, of the Mothers, home, etc. He is not happy because he is locked into a grid of responsibilities and duties working on a farm that is sapping the energy out of him, but he perks up when 3P0 mentions that he and R2 have seen battle. "You know of the Rebellion against the Empire?" he says, excitedly.

Luke is not a farmer, but due to the circumstances in which he has been raised, he has found himself trapped in a life without imagination. He is an idealist and a Romantic who dreams of faraway places and exotic lands and battles. The quixotic idea of rescuing a captured princess activates his imagination.

The message has come down to him—seemingly by accident--from the world of Light up above, the realm of the Spirit, and it has descended, following the trajectory of the droids from the escape pod to the dunes and then onward to the Jawas and then the sale of the droids to this farmer making a grim living who is always in a bad mood. It is analogous to the Manichean myth in which the Anthropos suits up in an armor of Light and descends down into the world of physical matter to do battle with the demons there, who end up eating his armor and trapping the Light in darkness.[20]

Luke, as his name suggests, is like a particle of light trapped in darkness who requires outside intervention to break him free from the external carapace of his duties and drudgeries in the Fourth House. The tiny princess is an earth goddess, but she is presented in this scene as a being made out of light who herself requires rescue and has sent a message down into the darkness of the physical material world to remind a grizzled old Jedi warrior--the last one living, as far as she knows--to come and get her. The message does eventually make its way to its intended destination, but along the way it is intercepted by a young boy whose entire world shifts seismically, as though Neptune, the god of earthquakes, had transited through his Fourth House.

The twins, both Luke and Leia, have been captured into their respective prisons, from which they require rescue: she from the overcoding of the sign regime of Empire, and Luke from his fall into the dull pragmatism of an ordinary everyday nine to five existence. Each will play a part in rescuing the other from their predicaments, but before that can happen, they will require the knowledge and wisdom of a Wise Old Man who, though he is too old to fight, will make use of Luke by proxy to perform the rescue for him.

The Escape of R2D2

(22:34 – 29:50)

There follows a series of very short, somewhat awkwardly directed scenes detailing the escape of R2D2, who is the first of these characters to break free of the various situations of confinement that all of the lead characters thus far have found themselves in.

During lunch with his aunt and uncle, Luke insists that he wants to join the Academy, but his uncle reiterates that he needs the extra help for the coming season's harvest. Luke tells him that he thinks R2D2 once belonged to an old man named Ben Kenobi, and his uncle tells him that Ben Kenobi died a long time ago and that Luke should just forget about it. He wants Luke to take the droids into Anchorhead the next morning in order to have their memories wiped and he promises—as he has promised for season after season—to let Luke go off on his own after the next harvest. Luke baulks and gets up from the table, depressed, as he wanders off to finish cleaning the droids. His aunt then reiterates to Uncle Owen that "Luke just isn't a farmer. He's got too much of his father in him," and Uncle Owen, knowing full well who Luke's real father was, tells her, "That's what I'm afraid of."

When Luke returns to the darkened tool shed he finds C3P0 hiding guiltily in the shadows, and the droid insists that though it wasn't his fault, R2 has gone—as a result of tricking Luke into removing his restraining bolt—babbling on about his "mission."

Luke scans the dusky horizon looking for him with a pair of binoculars, and when 3P0 asks whether they shouldn't go after him, Luke says, "It's too dangerous," for there are Sandpeople about at night. They'll have to wait until morning. It is, in fact, the last night of sheltering protection that Luke will ever experience.

The next morning, when Uncle Owen wakes up—his last--he asks Aunt Beru where Luke has gone and she tells him that he took the droids into Anchorhead like Owen asked him to do. Owen replies that if Luke isn't back in time to fix certain condenser units in the South Ridge by nightfall, then there will be hell to pay.

Luke, meanwhile, having taken C3P0 with him inside of his Landspeeder, races with it across the dusty ground through canyons, dried wadis and empty ravines. It is the first time we have seen him enter the dromosphere—Paul Virilio's term for the realm of speed[21]—and he is apparently quite comfortable within it. A group of ragged and dusty Sandpeople, however, spot him from their vantage point up in the hills and begin to organize at once to intercept him on their lumbering, shaggy Banthas.

Luke, then, having caught up with R2D2, jumps out of the speeder and asks him where he thinks he's going. He babbles to C3P0 yet again about his "mission," and while 3P0 makes apologies for him to Luke, R2 picks up a warning sign with his droid radar that there are other entities in the area. Sandpeople, Luke guesses, or something even worse. He grabs a weapon and his binoculars and tells 3P0 to follow him up to have a look down at the canyon. Through his binoculars he spots a pair of Banthas, and then makes out one of the Sandpeople standing guard beside the enormous beast, but at that moment his view is obstructed while one of them attacks him and knocks him unconscious, as C3P0 falls, screaming, over the cliff backwards.

R2 watches timidly from a cleft in the rocks while three Sandpeople raid the Landspeeder for booty, but they are startled when they hear a monstrous noise and see an ominous brown-garbed figure heading fearlessly down out of the hills toward them.

The essence of the entire sequence, then, captures Luke's birth exit from the Fourth House, the House of domesticity that is ruled by the sign of Cancer, a creature with an exoskeleton, and indeed, Luke has been living on the inside of a kind of exoskeleton: that, namely, of the childhood shelter of his aunt and uncle's home. By pursuing R2D2 on his way to deliver the message from Princess Leia, Luke is simultaneously—without knowing it—being ejected from the protective carapace of his Cancerian shell and now finds himself "thrown" into the world unprotected and vulnerable to assault.

Lacking the sheltering carapace of the Fourth House, Luke is now out *in* the world, where he very quickly finds himself on the Outside of Everything. It is the hostile encounter with the Other which marks the crucial transition from his childhood life of being protected by his foster parents to being exposed and vulnerable to attack from the hostile Other. The Sandpeople are nomadic tribesmen—disguised Berbers, let's say--whose camels have been swapped out for alien Banthas in Lucas's science fiction universe. They are the nomadic desert dwellers who exist in a perpetual state of being "unhomed," for as they roam the deserts, only the dome of the sky forms anything like a roof for them. They assault Luke *horizontally*, as it were, just as the droids have come down to him vertically from the heavens above. Their vertical line of descent towards his home, though, has had the effect of breaking him free from the Fourth House and its exoskeletal protection. Without them, he might've ended up like his uncle, perpetually stuck in the drudgery of the tasks required for daily survival and accordingly, always in a bad mood.

Instead, the droids have impacted his life like a meteor and caused a seismic shift in his circumstances which have had the effect of "Throwing" him, in Heideggerian fashion, out *into* the world, where he can then—finally—move on into the difficult work of mastering the tasks of the Sixth House, that, namely, of small animals.[22] The difficult tasks of that House, however, will require the encounter with a Master, which will help to shift him—eventually, although not in the present film—into the Seventh House—the House of Partners--where one stands on an equal footing with one's enemies.

That will not be achieved, however, until *Return of the Jedi*.

For now, he is on his way *out* of the pit that formed the architecture of his dwelling as an earth creature, and will climb slowly, ever so slowly, *upwards* to the realm of Light from whence the princess's message of distress has come. Thus, the downward vectors of the film's first half hour now begin to shift with the present scene, to upward vectors.

The droids have come tumbling down from out of the belly of a gigantic spaceship, and their erratic course has led them—thanks, largely, to R2's intuition—to the One who, with the name of "Skywalker," lives on the inside of a hole in the ground and therefore contains the potential for uniting both the heavenly world of Spirit with the earthly plane of Soul.

The film is thus structured with a hidden geometry around a central cosmic axis that it first moves *down*, then slides *up*. In the end, both vectors will unite with the liberation of the Princess from her captivity in the Tenth House, the House of the Father, which, of course, is the Death Star, an image of the earth itself overcoded and imprisoned within the global vectors of the Anti-World constructed by the value neutral and place-erasing architecture of corporate Big Science.

It should be noted that all of these worlds—Tatooine, the Death Star, Alderaan, etc.—are merely metaphors for various topographies of the earth itself. Lucas has simply created a topology of separating out the various problem zones of the contemporary globalized planet into their own separate "worlds," for in a sense, each one does constitute its own "world horizon" in Heideggerian fashion. Tatooine is simply the earth's desert zones, most of which occupy the same latitude—from the American Southwest at one end, going across North Africa, the Middle East and onward to the Gobi Desert at the other—separated off into its own world, as though it were a planet unto itself. The technologies and capitalist economics of globalization, on the other hand, constitute an Anti-World that is attempting to homogenize the planet so that all places are transformed into the same "No Place"—Kunstler's *Geography of Nowhere*[23] or Marc Auge's *Non-Places*[24]—which is completely opposed to the various unique and cultural specificities native to particular locales. Lucas has simply separated out that Anti-World and called it "the Empire," and, at least for the first film of his epic series, localized it to its own artificial planet called the Death Star. Hence, the ice world of Hoth in *The Empire Strikes Back* is simply the earth's northern frozen latitudes separated off as though they constituted their own world, and likewise with Dagobah—Yoda's home planet in the same film—as a jungle planet which corresponds to the earth's equatorial zones. The earth is composed of *all* of these zones, for no planet—unless it is a dead one, and there are plenty of those out there—is topologically homogenous.

Introduction of Ben Kenobi

(29:51 – 36:54)

The strange, brown-robed figure wearing a hood over his face now approaches and tends to Luke while he invites R2 to come out from his hiding place among the rocks. He removes his hood to reveal a gray-haired and bearded old man who assures R2 that Luke is just fine. When Luke comes to, he explains to the old man that R2 is looking for his former master, someone named Obi-Wan Kenobi. "Now that's a name I've not heard for a long time," says the old man and when Luke asks if he knows who R2 is talking about, the old man tells him that he himself is Obi-Wan Kenobi, though he has ceased using that name. The sounds of approaching Sandpeople get them scrambling quickly to get back inside, but first they must retrieve a fallen C3P0, who has lost his arm, from over the cliff edge.

In the following shot, Lucas gives the viewer a brief glimpse of Kenobi's house (this is in the 1997 version, which differs significantly from the original 1977 image): it has a dome on it, like Luke's tool shed, but Kenobi's dome is perched atop a rectangular shape and the house is on the edge of a cliff that overlooks a sea of dunes. The architectural morphology is important because it indicates that Kenobi has integrated *both* opposed orders: that of the round feminine uteromorphic order—the earth's etheric lines, in other words—as well as the angular world of technology, politics and the state apparatus that he has had to deal with during the days of the Republic. Luke's last name and his domestic origins from a hole in the ground, on the other hand, indicates that he has the *potential* to integrate both orders, but has to make his way through the lessons of the Sixth House, which is essentially Kenobi's home itself.

Inside the house, as Luke fixes C3P0's broken arm, he is in the midst of telling Kenobi that his father didn't fight in the Clone Wars but was a navigator on a spice freighter. Kenobi insists that that is what his uncle *wants* him to think, because his uncle wanted Luke's father to avoid the wars and become a farmer like himself. But Kenobi explains to him that Luke's father was also a Jedi knight, and that he fought along with him in the Clone Wars. Kenobi also tells him that he was a great star pilot, a cunning warrior and a good friend.

He is then reminded of something and crosses the room to open up an old wooden box, from whence he retrieves Luke's father's lightsaber and hands it to him. Luke turns it on and it sears into humming, pulsing blue light while Kenobi explains to him that his father wanted him to have it and that it is the weapon of a Jedi knight, an antique left over from a more civilized age.

The scene is, of course, a direct echo from Wagner's opera *Siegfried*, in which the dwarf Mimir, who has raised Siegfried as a fosterling, hands to him when he is old enough his father Sigmund's broken sword Nothung, which Siegfried then sets to work reforging anew. His task is to put the two fragmented pieces of the sword back together again.

Luke then tells Kenobi that he wishes he had known his father, and when he turns off the lightsaber and asks Ben how his father died, Kenobi replies that a young pupil of his named Darth Vader became seduced by the dark side of the Force and hunted down and murdered all the Jedi to extinction. He also betrayed and murdered Luke's father.

When Luke first hears this strange new word, "the Force," he asks Ben to explain it to him and Kenobi tells him that it is a mystical energy field that surrounds and penetrates all things. Most importantly, however, it gives to the Jedi his power and strength.

When R2 then beeps insistently, Kenobi stands and sets about the business of trying to fathom why R2 has sought him out, and it is at that moment that R2 projects the entire message programmed into him by the princess onto the little table in front of them. A fuzzy, blue-grainy Princess Leia addresses Ben directly and says that because he served her father years ago in the Clone Wars, she had been on her way to Tatooine to pick him up and bring him with her back to her home planet of Alderaan to help in the struggle against the Empire, but her ship was intercepted in the process.

After contemplating the tiny princess's message a moment, Kenobi insists that Luke must learn the mystic ways of the Force and accompany him to Alderaan to help the princess. But Luke baulks, claiming that he has too many obligations to do work for his uncle and that he wishes he could help fight the Empire but at this time is too bogged down with work to even consider it. He tells Ben that he could give him a lift to Anchorhead, from whence Kenobi could then hitch a ride on a transport to wherever he wants to go, but that's about the best he can do for him.

Kenobi tells him, patiently, that he must do what he thinks is right, of course.

In this scene, Kenobi gives to Luke the necessary tools to integrate the two orders which he himself, as a Jedi master, has already long since mastered: the orders of angular thinking as opposed to curvilinear thinking; the masculine technological and the female-mystical; the local and particular with the universal. The lightsaber is, of course, the Lacanian phallus, recovered here by Luke—who has been castrated of all his power by the web of his uncle's lies—which will enable him to interact with the cosmic-uteromorphic structure of the Force, a mystical energy field of etheric lines of force that shape the morphology of an Einsteinian curvilinear universe. The Force is feminine, the lightsaber its masculine and particular servant: the saber, that is, draws power from the female energy of the Force—which is known in Indian philosophy as *shakti*, which has a feminine valency—and channels it to a specific *point* in space / time where the Jedi wishes to apply its universal-cosmic energy. But first one must become the servant of the energy—of the womb-sphere of what Jean Gebser termed the magical consciousness structure,[25] which envisions the universe as a single point-like unity best expressed architecturally in the form of the cavern—and *then* once the servant has plugged himself umbilically into the etheric energy lines of the Force, he can use the lightsaber-as-Phallus to direct universal energies to specific points that act as extensions of his will. He himself thus becomes an extension of cosmic energy and power, just as the Shiva lingam channels the power and energy of *shakti*.

So in place of Siegfried's broken sword, Lucas here presents us with a series of fragments and disjunctions that it will be Luke's task to unify and integrate: the local and the global; the technological and the mystical; the angular and the curvilinear; the singular and the universal.

Standing inside of Ben Kenobi's house, Luke has already

left behind the Fourth House—that of his aunt and uncle—
and entered into the Sixth, for Kenobi's house *is* the House
of Small Animals which Luke as his pupil must now learn
to master in order to stand on his own against the opposing
powers of the Twelfth House, that, namely of the Big
Animals: archetypes and institutions.

In the process, he will liberate the captured earth goddess,
just as in *The Ramayana*, when his beloved Sita (whose name
means "furrow") is abducted by the demon Ravana, Rama
must—with the aid of an army of monkeys—rescue her from
the demon fortress on the island of Sri Lanka by building a
vast wooden bridge that connects the Indian peninsula with
the island. In that story, the Small Animals are the monkeys
that help Rama stand on a one-to-one footing with the
demon Ravana.

Luke has a big task ahead of him: in place of constructing
a wooden bridge horizontally across the waters connecting
two continents, he must construct a ladder of ascent that
will lead him from the earth and the particularities of his
specific location upon it, to the heavens, where he will deal
with the universal energies of the Spirit.

Introduction of the Death Star
(36:55 – 39:04)

A shot of the Imperial Star Destroyer heading for the Death Star now follows. For a few seconds, the viewer is shown the round gray globe of an enormous battle station that appears to be the size of a planet. The Star Destroyer heading towards it is presumably the same one from the film's opening sequence, now carrying the captured princess to her prison. The uteromorphic globe, as I have already pointed out, is tantamount to the Empire's encasing of the earth *inside* of a techno-skeleton of beaming signals and roving satellites, radar systems, missile guidance, etc. (the image was possibly inspired by Isaac Asimov's vision of the city of Trantor in his *Foundation* novels, a city which Asimov describes as coterminous with the entire surface of the planet).

The next shot takes place inside one of the space station's administrative conference rooms, where officials wearing tan and gray outfits are seated at an ebony round table that ironically echoes King Arthur's round table. Whereas the film's color palette up to this point has been dominated largely by earth tones—coffee-brown sand dunes, copper-colored cliffs, etc.—everything inside the conference room of the Death Star is now gray and colorless. The overall impression is of a world that has been denuded of all color, the vitality drained out of it by imperial bureaucratic and technical systems of control. Indeed, it looks like any conference room inside the glossy offices of some monolithic transnational corporation, where intellect, together with its angular thinking, has completely taken control and all of the earth's biormorphic forces and energies have been walled out. The circular shape of the conference table reiterates the capturing of all geo-morphic and feminine semiotics by the Empire.

Two of the officials seated at the table are having a dispute about the battle station: one of them maintains that until it is fully operational, the rebels will prove to be too dangerous, while his opponent insists that the danger will be only to the man's fleet, not to the Death Star itself. The fleet commander is in the middle of pointing out that the rebellion will continue to gain support from the Imperial Senate when Darth Vader and the station's commander, a man named Grand Moff Tarkin (played by Peter Cushing) both stride into the room. Tarkin cuts the man off in mid-sentence when he announces that the Imperial Senate has now been completely dissolved by the Emperor, and when one of the officials asks how it would be possible for the Emperor to control his Empire without the necessary bureaucratic apparatus, Tarkin tells him that the territories are now under the control of regional governors. Tarkin insists that fear of the Death Star will keep the local regions under control. It is an age, in other words, that typically occurs in civilizations when they form Universal States[26] in which the creative elite of a society has shifted to a dominant minority, who lead now by fear and intimidation and no longer through creatively inspiring the masses with playful artistic imitation and religious ritual.

The official then counters by pointing out that if the rebels have obtained the technical plans of the battle station, then it is possible that they could find a weakness to exploit it, but at this point Vader speaks up and points out that the stolen plans will soon be back in their hands.

One of the other officials claims that any attack made upon the battle station by the rebels would be a useless gesture since it is now the most powerful thing in the universe. Darth Vader, mildly offended by this hubristic faith in mere technological monstrosities, points out that the station's power is nothing compared to the mystical powers of the Force and when the man counters by pointing out that the powers of the Force have not given Vader the ability to find the rebellion's secret location or to obtain the stolen battle plans, Vader raises his hand and activates an invisible energy noose around the man's neck that begins choking him. "I find your lack of faith disturbing," says Vader while Tarkin tells them to quit bickering and release the man, to which Vader accedes.

Tarkin then assures them all that Vader will soon provide them with the location of the rebel fortress by the time the battle station is fully operational. And then the rebellion will be simply crushed and wiped out.

Thus, the scene performs the function of contrasting the semiotics of the Empire with those of the rebellion, for it all takes place inside the completely mechanized and artificial world of the Death Star, where angular thinking and militaristic hi-technologies have become dominant. The signifiers associated with the rebellion, by contrast, are always in some manner earthly, for the rebels are always hiding out in natural environments like jungles, deserts and forests, where they remain in touch with geo- and bio-morphic forces.

The earth, speaking metaphorically, is *inside* the Death Star, just as Anakin Skywalker is *inside* the exoskeletal suit of Darth Vader, which keeps him alive. The princess, too, has now been captured and placed on the *inside* of the Death Star.

The rebellion and its various characters, on the other hand, are all on the *outside*, where they are exposed to the earth's invisible morphic energy fields which require the knowledge and skill of a Jedi knight to show them how to allow those fields to guide them.

The state and technological apparatus of the Death Star war machine wants to swallow everything and everyone, to put it all on the *inside* of technical systems which have assumed control over, and are designed as artificial replacements, for natural powers.

Star Wars is the epic poetry of a late cosmopolitan civilization in which technology, business and science have gained the upper hand over art, culture and spirituality, which includes the powers of the land itself, with all its agrarian traditions, local rituals and folk piety. Art and culture are produced in particular towns not yet dominated by such Big Systems, and in which things, as Heidegger puts it, are still capable of "thinging," that is to say, of resonating with the authentic aura of their historical and natural locality.[27] The authentically produced art object, as Walter Benjamin pointed out (and here he comes surprisingly close to Heidegger, despite their being far left and far right politically speaking) contains an aura of site-specific authenticity that the world of global trans-national commerce effaces and annihilates with all its Big Systems and technological means of mass reproduction. It is the authenticity of particular *Ereignis* events—unprecedented "turnings" of art, you might say—that such Big Systems threaten to wipe out.[28] Hence, when Tarkin insists that the rebellion will be crushed by the powers of the Empire and its Death Star, this is precisely what he is maintaining: namely, that there will no longer exist a world in which *Ereignis* events of cultural authenticity take place any longer, for all art, in such Universal States, becomes state appropriated and controlled. Nothing is allowed to happen that the state itself does not authorize—and this is just as true for totalitarian regimes on the Far Left (i.e. Stalinism) as it is for those on the Far Right (i.e. the Nazis).

The Deaths of Uncle Owen
and Aunt Beru
(39:05 – 40:54)

In this scene, Luke and Ben have come across the ruins of a Sandcrawler with the dead bodies of massacred Jawas strewn all about the ground around it. Luke says that the attack must have been done by Sandpeople, for there are gaffi sticks lying about (weapons normally carried by Sandpeople), but he has never heard of them hitting anything so large before as a Sandcrawler. Ben tells him that it *wasn't* Sandpeople, but that it was made to look as if it were. The Bantha tracks imprinted into the ground indicate animals travelling side by side whereas Sandpeople always travel single file to conceal their numbers, he says. He also points out that the blast points are too accurate to have been made by Sandpeople, but that only Imperial stormtroopers could have done this.

When Luke wonders aloud why stormtroopers would attack Jawas, he realizes that it was the same group of Jawas that sold the droids to his aunt and uncle. And that means they would've been able to figure out precisely to whom the droids were sold, which would lead the stormtroopers back to Luke's home.

At once, he jumps into his Landspeeder, heedless of Kenobi's warning that it might be too dangerous, and when he arrives at his house, he is confronted with a smoking, charred ruin. The still smoldering bodies of his aunt and uncle are lying near the doorway to the tool shed, their flesh seared completely away to reveal their skeletons beneath.

Luke now has no home to return to.

The scene, as is well known, is an homage to John Ford's classic Western *The Searchers*, in which Ethan (played by John Wayne) returns to his homestead to find that his entire family has been massacred by Comanche Indians.[29]

But in the present instance, the semiotics are very different, for the scene represents the final threshold crossing for Luke that shifts him out of the prison of responsibilities as a farmer that he had been raised in—the Fourth House in astrology—and prepares to move him into the Sixth House, that, namely, of the mastery of "small animals." Because he could not make the decision to abandon the life of a farmer to become a Jedi knight on his own, Fate made the decision for him and acted through the Imperial stormtroopers as a wedge to shift him out of the house of his childhood and move him on the way into a new adulthood.

It is very much as though the Egg encasing him has cracked open and he has emerged from it, unhomed, with the shell lying in pieces all about him. Ontologically speaking, he is now "homeless," unprotected by the shell of his Cancerian exoskeleton. He has crawled up from out of the pit house that he was raised in, having come directly up from the earth itself, and is now ready to begin his upward climb to the domain of the realm of Spirit, a very much larger reality that includes the order of Lacan's Big Other and the shifting masks of Jung's various personae.

To reiterate: the vector guiding the droids has been an arc of descent; but the vector tracking out Luke's current path is one of ascent, moving in the opposite direction.

From henceforth, every step he takes will be a step *upward* toward the realm from whence the beings of light and spirit have come down to him.

At the film's inception, Princess Leia's little starship had been on its way to Tatooine to fish Ben Kenobi out from the Waste Land and carry him with her to Alderaan, but because she was captured along the way, she had to send, in place of her physical self, a miniaturized avatar of light. But the bait was spectacularly successful, for she managed to catch *two* fish, instead of one, for Ben Kenobi *and* Luke Skywalker are the missing signifiers necessary to complete two binary sets of twins: Kenobi will slide into the semiotic vacancy in opposition to his old nemesis, Darth Vader; while Luke is Leia's long-lost twin brother that she never knew she had. But since Kenobi is too old and worn out with years of battle fatigue—and presumably some form of PTSD—he will require Skywalker as a biological extension of himself, renewed and young once again, to complete the task for him.

The Torture of Princess Leia

(40:55 – 41:40)

Three Imperial T.I.E. fighters—polished gray-black—are now shown heading for the Death Star as a transitional shot to the space station. Meanwhile, inside one of the Death Star's corridors, Darth Vader is shown walking purposefully forward, escorted by two Imperial guards. The corridor is completely black, with a reddish lattice grille floor. They pause in front of a room, the door to which slides instantly open, and Vader steps down into Princess Leia's prison chamber. It is a small room with black walls and a glowing red grille ceiling. The Princess, thus far, looks unharmed, but as Vader steps toward her he says that they will now begin the process of discussing the location of the rebel fortress. Behind him, through the doorway, there floats a sinister-looking black ball with chromium features and various instruments poking from its surface, one of which, as the camera closes in, appears to be a hypodermic needle, possibly loaded with sodium pentothal or some other kind of "truth serum." The probe floats forward into the room, making a pulsating electronic hum, and the door slides shut.

Thus far the film has shown us various characters in situations of confinement. The capture, first, of Princess Leia; followed by the capture and sale of the droids; and

Luke's discontent as an unhappy farmer dreaming of a more exotic life as an adventurer. R2D2 was the first to trace a line of flight out of his imprisonment when Luke removed his restraining bolt, and the pursuit of R2 eventually led to the dislodging of Luke from his own confinement to the life of a farmer. This release from his own prison, however, was effected by the murder of his foster parents, but he is now free and on his way to begin his journey through the cosmos.

The present scene, on the other hand, shows us, for the first time, the claustrophobic nature of Princess Leia's confinement in a small prison cell inside the Death Star. The situation is made even worse by the sight of the torture probe that now moves towards her with the needle out and ready.

Vader will try—unsuccessfully, as it turns out—to torture the secret of the location of the rebel fortress out of her. But the scene can also be read as a process of inscription: that is, the needle can function just as well—as one does, for instance, in Kafka's short story "In the Penal Colony," in which one's crimes are inscribed by such a machine into the flesh—as an instrument of inscription to begin the process of overcoding the princess with the Imperial sign regime. She is not just going to be tortured: but rather, also, "overcoded" by the semiotics of the state apparatus and its biopolitics. The electronic tagging, inscribing with RFID chips and other such means of branding by the state apparatus are biopolitical forms of inscription which encode the individual into the System so that he or she can be tracked and monitored like human cattle. One's "rights" under such conditions dissolve into thin air as the state strips away all forms of protection. The princess, in other words, has no protective exoskeleton to prevent her from being stripped down to the level of what Giorgio Agamben called *zoe*, or bare naked life, in which individuals are stripped of their rights as the state withdraws its juridical, protective shell, or encasing from them. They can then be put into camps, where they can be tortured or killed with impunity, such as is presently the case at Guantanomo Bay.[30]

Whereas Luke's protective carapace has just been stripped from him by the death of his foster parents, Princess Leia has also had her protective shell of "diplomatic" rights stripped from her and she is now reduced ontologically to the status of "bare naked life." Anything can be done to her, and nobody need be held responsible for her fate.

She is pure pink flesh, exposed, uncoded, unprotected and unhomed.

But the process of inscribing her into the state apparatus is now about to begin.

Mos Eisley Spaceport
(41:41 – 47:28)

When Luke returns in his Landspeeder to the ruined Sandcrawler where Ben and the droids are burning the dead bodies of the Jawas, Ben explains to him that there was nothing he could have done to save his aunt and uncle. Luke himself would most likely be dead and the droids would've ended up in the hands of the Empire. Luke then tells Ben that he wants to travel with him to Alderaan, after all, and that he also wishes to learn the ways of the Force and become a Jedi knight like his father. Ben nods his assent and in the next shot, they are speeding away across the tan and copper desert. They come to a stop at the edge of a cliff and get out, where they have a panoramic view of Mos Eisley Spaceport, which can be glimpsed in the bare topographical distance as a glittering series of buildings with tiny spaceships taking off and landing like wasps. Ben tells Luke, however, that he will never find a more wretched hive of scum and villainy than at Mos Eisley.

The 1997 version of the film now contains perhaps its least successful CGI add-in with a sequence that follows, showing Ben, Luke and the droids entering the fringes of the spaceport in a video-gamey-looking Landspeeder as they pass some scurrying womp rats and a pair of droids that get into a brief, and needlessly silly, altercation. The camera pans back to reveal an expanded view of Mos Eisley, but the graphics are of a kind of aesthetic kitsch that is barely distinguishable from those of hi-tech video games like *Call of Duty* or *Grand Theft Auto*. The city in this shot has a flat, fake low-resolution look to it that appears slightly unfinished, perhaps.

The city, nevertheless, swarms with robots, Jawas, aliens and, in the 1997 edition, dinosaurish creatures that look as though they were borrowed from *Jurassic Park*. The speeder is stopped by a detachment of four stormtroopers, who question them about how long they've owned their droids. When they ask for identification, Ben, using a subtle mind trick on them, tells them, like a hypnotist, that they don't need to see his identification. The stormtrooper, as though in a trance, repeats the line, and when Ben tells him that these aren't the droids they're looking for, another stormtrooper repeats what Ben says. The stormtrooper then tells them to move along.

The speeder pulls up in front of a crumbling, sun-baked cantina with a domical-shaped roof. Most of the buildings, in fact—as is consistent with much of North African architecture, where the desert scenes were filmed—have dome-shaped roofs that look old, and well-worn: composed of adobe and mud-brick, they have rusty, water-stained patches leaking down their aged sides.

Luke tells Ben that he can't understand how they got past the stormtroopers, but Kenobi explains to him that the Force can have a strong influence on the weak-minded. Luke then asks, with a certain degree of skepticism, whether Ben actually thinks they can find a pilot capable of taking them all the way to Alderaan, but Ben reassures him that most of the best freighter pilots *can* be found here, but he also warns him to watch his step and that the place can be a little rough.

Inside, the cantina is dark and poorly lit, with a band playing faintly Jazz-sounding music in the background. At the tables are seated creatures and aliens from various exotic worlds with bizarre features that look as though they had been borrowed from the pages of *Barlowe's Guide to Extraterrestrials* (although that book came out in 1979). While Ben Kenobi is referred by another pilot to Chewbacca, who towers behind him, the bartender informs Luke to keep his droids outside.

While Luke edges his way to the bar, and Kenobi is busy negotiating with Chewbacca to his right, a creature with a walrus-looking face approaches Luke aggressively from his left and growls something at him in an alien language. His sidekick, a man with a deformed face, taps Luke on the shoulder and tells him that the walrus-man doesn't like him. He also informs Luke that *he* doesn't like him, either, and that he'd better watch himself since he is dealing with wanted men. Luke insists that he'll be careful and tries to mind his own business when the man yells, "You'll be dead!" and shoves him backwards. Kenobi, noticing the commotion, turns away from Chewbacca and offers to buy the man a drink, but the man insists upon violence and reaches for his blaster. Within seconds, Kenobi's humming blue lightsaber is out and slashes the man's arm off at the shoulder. The saber disappears just as quickly, and the cantina music resumes as Kenobi helps Luke to get up from the floor.

The essence of the entire scene is to form the liminal transition from the local to the global and international. Mos Eisley is a shabby, particular example of the global Anti-World, together with all its Non-Places, as Marc Auge has defined them: that is to say, these are places, like airports, hotels, gas stations, convenience stores and shopping malls, that are designed for people to *move through* rather than to inhabit for any great length of time. Unlike the world of Old Europe, with all its historically authentic palaces, churches and cathedrals, Non-Places have no "aura" about them and no cultural authenticity. They are strictly designed as temporal structures to serve merely functional purposes, and they are part of the infrastructure of the global Anti-World of capitalism.

In the present instance, Luke and Ben have entered into a Zone of Otherness where alien beings, functioning as signifiers pointing to Other Worlds, are all gathered together at a single place. Multiple worlds, that is to say, with multiple ethnicities all here jostle and crowd together, each signifying a nodal entry point from whence the narrative could branch off into any other of these many worlds. It is a little like Borges's short story, "The Garden of Forking Paths" in which all narrative possibilities co-exist simultaneously.

All these aliens have a special ontological status about them in that they have been de-worlded from their proper native habitats. The spaceport therefore is a kind of public structure for the momentary habitation of deworlded entities which exist in the mode of Heidegger's *Vorhandenheit*. That is to say, they are entities torn free from their cultural contexts—in self-sufficient mode, like Lucretius's atoms— jostling together and rubbing elbows. The friction that results whenever particular nodal spots upon topographical maps that allow such entities to gather often results in violence.

The spaceport is also a place where local entities— places that function like our contemporary airports—can be removed from their particular horizons and thrown into circulation about the planet's global ecumene. At such places, the local is *lifted up* and transformed into a floating, de-worlded signifier, just as today such de-worlded communities find themselves thriving around the globe:

London, for instance, has the largest Muslim community in Europe. The best Chinese food might not be found in China anymore, but in San Francisco or New York. Mosques are, today, found everywhere, just as are Greek Orthodox churches. It is an age, as theoretician Boris Groys has pointed out, of de-worlded signifiers which are in circulation across the entire planet.[31]

Airports--and in the semiotics of science fiction "spaceports"--are precisely the nodal points where the de-localizing of such entities takes place. It is a Zone of Otherness where violence is always on the verge of erupting because so many different worlds have been compacted and compressed into one topographical locale. Hence, Luke's confrontation with the stranger who doesn't like him, for no particular reason beyond his Otherness.

But it is also a threshold crossing. It is a "spaceport" and as such, functions as a kind of technological staircase upon which the vectors of the narrative now begin to move "upward." Luke's very presence there is a step upward from Ben's house, which, in turn, had been a step upward out of the pit of his aunt and uncle's home. The film's vectors have, to this point, traced the downward trajectory of the droids and their message of Light from the World Above. At Mos Eisley, the downward pointing arrow—like one of those huge arrows painted by Paul Klee—shifts its direction to an upward pointing arrow.

At Mos Eisley, *both* arrows are gathered together in a kind of Star of David or Shri Yantra that is composed of intersecting arrows gathering Soul and Spirit into one spot.

The *Millennium Falcon*, as the ship's name implies, will become the mechanical Garuda bird that will carry Luke upwards to the realm of Light, and outwards into the vast expanses of the masculine world of Spirit and all its global encompassing constructions---the Death Star, Imperial Star Destroyers, etc.

Introduction of Han Solo

(47:29 – 51:12)

Ben now tells Luke that he has been talking with Chewbacca—a tall, furry mammalian creature that resembles a cross between a dog and a monkey—who happens to be first mate on a ship that might be able to take them to Alderaan. They sit down at a corner table where Chewbacca seats himself beside Han Solo, who introduces himself to Ben and Luke as the captain of the *Millenium Falcon*. When the two seem unimpressed and Ben inquires whether they are supposed to have heard of the ship, Solo tells them that it's the ship that made the Kessel Run in less than 12 parsecs. When Ben, still unimpressed, says that they want to avoid any Imperial entanglements, Solo tells him that that is tricky and will therefore cost them extra. He quotes the price of 10,000 (though the currency is never specified by Lucas) to the indignation of Luke who claims that they could almost buy their own spaceship for that much money. Solo counters by asking him if he could pilot it, and Luke insists that he is not such a bad pilot and probably could. As he is about to stand up and walk away, telling Ben that they don't need to listen to Solo's nonsense, Ben firmly pulls him back down and tells Solo that they can pay him 2,000 now and another 15,000 when they reach Alderaan. Solo likes the sound of earning 17,000 for a mere charter run, so he agrees and tells them that his ship is located at docking bay 94.

When Solo looks over Ben's shoulder and sees Imperial stormtroopers inquiring about the recent violence in the café—they are like Roman soldiers in Judaea during late Maccabean times always on the alert for potential revolts--he notifies Ben that it looks like someone has taken an interest in his handiwork. In the next scene, as two stormtroopers pass by their table, Ben and Luke have vanished, and only Solo and Chewbacca are seated casually, sipping their drinks.

When the stormtroopers wander away, Solo tells Chewbacca that 17,000 is a lot of money and could really dig him out of the hole he is in—and note here that we are introduced to yet another protagonist who is caught in a situation of confinement--for he owes a creature named Jabba the Hut a lot of money. He says that Ben and Luke must really be desperate to offer to pay that much and tells Chewbacca to go ready the ship.

As Solo himself is about to get up, a green-headed, reptilian creature known as Greedo interrupts him, pointing a blaster at him, and forces him to sit back down. Greedo tells him that Jabba is very unhappy with him for evading his debt, but Solo insists that he now has the money he owes him, although he doesn't currently have it on him. Greedo suggests that if he gives the money to him directly, then he might forget about having found him. He also informs Solo that Jabba the Hut has put a huge price on his head that will be very attractive to bounty hunters. He tells Solo, that if he is lucky, Jabba will only take his ship and Solo tells him that that will happen "over my dead body." Greedo says that is exactly the idea and that he has been waiting for this for a very long time.

In the original theatrical release, Solo was shown firing first, but in the 1997 altered version, Greedo can clearly be seen shooting first, in accordance with the "softening" and "suburbanizing" tendencies of film in the late 1990s, when all its "dangerous" elements were in the process of being removed. Such a morally questionable character that would be implicated by having Han Solo fire his blaster, not in self-defense, but as an act of Clint Eastwood / Dirty Harry style aggression, is no longer permitted in the Hollywood cinema of the late 1990s.

Solo stands up and offers a coin to the bartender and apologizes for the mess.

The first point to note here is that there is an alliance formed, via Chewbacca, with the mammalian against the Empire, the semiotics of which are always associated—as I have remarked above—with either exoskeletal or reptilian creatures. There is a brief scene in this sequence in which the droids, waiting outside the cantina, watch a stormtrooper dismount from his reptilian beast, whereupon C3P0 remarks, watching as the stormtrooper enters the café, that he does not like the look of this.

So, just as in *The Ramayana*, in which the hero Rama forms an alliance with the king of the monkeys, Hanuman, to build a bridge from southern India to Sri Lanka, where the demon Ravana has his fortress and Rama's beautiful wife Sita imprisoned inside it, so here, the alliance with Chewbacca to build a bridge—not horizontally between land masses—but vertically, from the earth to the Death Star, indicates the more highly evolved nature of the rebels and the Jedi knights.

Also, in this scene an assemblage is formed that links the three humans together with one animal, which reverses the semiotics of the vision of Ezekiel, wherein he sees a so-called "tetramorph" at each corner of the heavenly chariot (Ez. 1:4), that is to say, a four-faced creature, in the Biblical case, a beast with three animal faces and one human that is powering the chariot. Later, in the Medieval construction of the Western zodiac, the signifiers of Ezekiel's vision--an ox, a lion, an eagle and a man--were associated with the Four Evangelists and were also linked with four fixed—that is to say, "middle"--signs of the zodiac: the Evangelist Luke with Taurus; Mark with Leo; John with an eagle that swaps out for Scorpio; and Matthew with the only human figure of the tetramorph, that namely, of Aquarius, the Water-Bearer.

In the present scene in *Star Wars*, however, the semiotics of the tradition of Ezekiel and the Evangelists is reversed, for now there are three *human* visages—Ben, Luke and Han Solo—with *one* animal, and a mammalian animal at that, vaguely resembling a dog hybridized with a monkey. The evolution of consciousness, in other words, has chosen to develop the "human" function with the overcoding of the earth by the creation of the frontal lobe's mechanical constructs, while leaving the animal, who is still in touch with the earth, behind; paved over, as it were, by the roads and GPS signals of the hypermodern "Death Star."

In battling the Empire, the animal function must be retrieved and carried along with the four as an essential signifier of earthly powers, just as Luke himself has come up from out of the earth and therefore represents its resistance to the Heideggerian "enframing" of the planet by technology.[32] The four characters—Ben, Luke, Han Solo and Chewbacca—now serve to construct the narrative's primary mandala of four differentiated functions that will create a tetramorphic assemblage as its narrative Subject. The four of them *together*, that is to say, are now a complete and single unified Subject. (Later, with the rescue of Princess Leia, she will be traded out for Ben Kenobi, who is killed at just about the same time she is rescued and joins the assemblage).

And this, despite Han Solo's status—as his name, "solo," as in "flying solo," indicates—as a lone floating signifier who prides himself on connecting with *no* assemblages whatsoever. But this failure to connect with any other assemblages—whether that represented by the Empire or the Rebellion—is precisely what has gotten him into so much trouble with gangsters like Jabba the Hut. He is always trying to fend for himself, with no one's help other than that of his animal sidekick Chewbacca, and as a result he is always in debt and in trouble with just about everybody he meets. But the pair of protagonists, i.e. Ben and Luke, whom he has just met, have already—unknown to his conscious mind—plugged him into a fourfold tetramorphic assemblage. For whether he knows it or not, he can no longer operate on his own. He is part of an assemblage that has unconsciously "clicked" together long before his conscious mind ever catches up and becomes aware that he has, in fact, already joined the Rebellion against the Empire.

Jabba the Hut

(51:13 – 54:12)

There is, once again, a transitional shot to the interior of the Death Star, this time with two T.I.E. fighters shown roaring past its gray, colorless exterior. Inside, Darth Vader is explaining to the Grand Moff Tarkin that Princess Leia's resistance to the mind probe has proved considerable. When an administrative official then steps up and informs Tarkin that the Death Star is now fully operational and asks what course they should set, Tarkin has an idea and suggests that perhaps Leia will respond to a more aggressive course of action if they threaten to destroy her home planet, Alderaan, and so he tells his officials to set their course for that planet.

The droids, meanwhile, down on Mos Eisley, are shown locking themselves inside of a utility closet as a group of four stormtroopers come walking up the street and knock on the door. When they realize that it is locked, they move on to the next one (note that the four stormtroopers form a counter-assemblage to the four protagonists, Ben, Luke, Han Solo and Chewbacca).

Luke is then shown selling his Landspeeder and complains to Ben that ever since the XP-38's came out, his model just hasn't been in demand. Kenobi assures him, however, that they will have enough. A dark, shrouded figure, meanwhile, with an elongated proboscis, is shown closely following behind them.

There follows, in the 1997 version of the film, a restored scene that was filmed for the original theatrical release that used a human actor as a stand-in to play the role of what was supposed to have been a stop-motion animated Jabba the Hut. Because of budgetary and time constraints, however, the scene was never completed, but it has been restored in the 1997 version using a CGI construct of Jabba the Hut, a slimy larval-looking creature who suggests a lower life form, a more devolved, worm-like being whose interests and motivations are strictly monetary.

The character of the bounty hunter named Boba Fett has also been added to the scene on the right hand side, a character who had, in the original trilogy, only made his first appearance in *The Empire Strikes Back*. This serves as a wonderful foreshadowing to the climax of *The Empire Strikes Back*, for it will be precisely Boba Fett who is given Han Solo by the Empire to return him to Jabba the Hut to collect his bounty.

Han is shown standing with his hand near his blaster from a low hip-shot point of view that reminds one of a shoot-out in an old Western. He tells Jabba that he has been waiting for him, and Jabba skeptically replies, "Have you now?" Solo insists that he had no plans to run from him, but when Jabba asks him why he fried poor Greedo, Solo tells him that next time he wants to talk with him, he should come himself instead of sending one of his "twerps." Jabba tells him that he can make no exceptions, and asks, rhetorically, what he would do if every smuggler he hired to carry contraband for him dropped his load at the first sign of an Imperial starship? Solo insists that even *he* gets boarded sometimes, and as he asks Jabba if he thinks he had a choice, steps on his tail as he circumnavigates to the other side of him. Solo tells him that he has a new, easy charter that will enable him to pay him back, and when Jabba insists upon a twenty percent cut, Solo becomes indignant and tells him not to push it, insisting on fifteen, to which Jabba agrees, but he warns Solo that if he fails to deliver the goods he'll put a huge price on his head. As Solo nears the entrance ramp to the *Millenium Falcon*, he tells Jabba, with some irony, that he is a good human being.

Jabba collects his gangsters and they clear out of the docking bay.

Jabba the Hut belongs to an ethnicity known as "the Huts," who are a group of gangsters native to the planet Tatooine, as we learn in other films like *Return of the Jedi* and *The Phantom Menace*. He resembles, as I have said, a lower worm-like life form—indeed he reminds one of the pink and flagellating creatures shown in the Origins of Life sequence in Terrence Malick's 2011 film *The Tree of Life*—and he may be inspired by the over-weight gangster named "Gutman" in the 1941 film of Dashiell Hammett's novel *The Maltese Falcon*. In my essay on that novel—which can be found in my recent book *Gods & Heroes of the Media Age*[33]—I there compared Gutman to a snake, for a snake is essentially a travelling "gut" or alimentary canal, in opposition to the bird motif of the Maltese Falcon idol itself, which forms the object of desire in that film.

Lucas's naming of Han Solo's ship, the *Millenium Falcon*, is most certainly an homage to that film, and the ship, in this scene, is clearly visible behind Han and Jabba. So the semiotics of the bird and the snake are present here in disguised form as a worm-like gangster and a spaceship that will function like a flying bird that will carry the protagonists out of the gravitational well of the planet of Tatooine, thus liberating Luke from his prison once and for all. Jabba, however, represents the opposing earthly element—the lower depths, let's say—of the intestinal system and the earth and its gravitational pull that has captured not only Luke but also Han, who remains psychologically imprisoned by his debt to Jabba even as his spaceship leaves Tatooine behind. Whereas Luke will finally be freed, Solo carries his prison with him wherever he goes, and he is not finally released from it until the prologue of *Return of the Jedi*, when Jabba is strangled to death by Princess Leia.

Flight from the Desert Planet
(54:13 – 57:00)

In the next scene, Ben tells Luke that if Han's ship is as fast as he boasts that it is, then they should do all right. They walk forward to meet Chewbacca, who waits for them at the entrance to the docking bay. Meanwhile, the shadowy figure with the long proboscis is following at a safe distance behind them and he is muttering something in an alien language into a communication device that he holds in his palm.

As Ben, Luke and the droids, meanwhile, enter the docking bay, they get a clear look at the *Millenium Falcon* for the first time: a flat round disc turned onto its side horizontally. Luke calls it a piece of junk, but Han, standing near the entrance ramp, reassures them that it will make .5 past lightspeed. He tells them he's made a lot of special modifications, but that they need to get onboard quickly.

Back inside the spaceport, meanwhile, the creature with the long proboscis informs a group of stormtroopers which docking bay the droids together with Ben and Luke have gone through, and their troop leader tells them to load their weapons. They go through the narrow entrance to the docking bay, where Han Solo happens to be putting a few finishing touches to some mechanical problem on the ship's exterior when a stormtrooper yells at him to stop the ship and orders his cohorts to blast them.

Han fires his blaster back at them a few times, doing considerable damage to the bay as chunks of debris crumble from the ceiling. He tells Chewie to get them out quickly as he runs aboard the ship, where Chewie is already in the co-pilot's seat, firing up the engines. Ben, Luke and the droids strap themselves in around a gaming table and C3P0 emphasizes how much he hates space travel.

An exterior shot of the *Falcon* lifting up out of the spaceport and gunning its engines to a soft blue-white then follows. Stormtroopers on the ground below look up to see the ship escaping, and in the next shot, from outer space, the *Millenium Falcon* is shown fleeing from the planet's gravitational well as its giant coppery disc surrounded with a faint blue halo recedes behind them.

Two Imperial Star Destroyers, however, have spotted them and begin pursuit, causing Han to tell Chewie that his passengers must be "hotter" than they'd let on. He tells him to make the calculations for the jump to hyperspace, as Ben and Luke step into the seats behind them, thus reforming their tetramorphic "assemblage."[34] Luke asks why Han can't seem to outrun the Imperial ships and Han snaps back that he'd better watch his mouth or else find himself floating back home.

The arrow-shaped white metal Imperial starships are shown closing in on the tiny disc of the falcon, shooting green laser blasts at it as they zero in. Han insists, though, that he knows a few maneuvers to outrun them.

Ben asks, with some nervousness, how long it will take them to make the jump to lightspeed, and Han says that it will take a few moments to make the correct calculations. "Are you kidding?" Luke says, "At the rate they're gaining?"

Han tells him that travelling through hyperspace isn't like dusting crops but a complex operation that requires precise calculations, otherwise the ship might bounce into a planet or a star and disintegrate.

Han tells Ben and Luke to go strap themselves in as he proceeds to make the jump to lightspeed. As the two recede back to their places around the gaming table, Han throws a switch and the ship bursts into lightspeed as the stars transform into geodesic lightpaths all around them.

It is, of course, a physical impossibility for any object to travel at the speed of light, but the metaphor has been taken from the *Foundation* novels of Isaac Asimov, in which ships travel through space by making what Asimov terms "the Jump into hyperspace."[35] The metaphor, though, suffices to emphasize their momentary escape from the clutches of the Empire.

Thus, the *Millenium Falcon* is a disguised bird upon the back of which its protagonists are carried out of the gravitational well of the planet Tatooine. The falcon was a bird sacred to the ancient Egyptians, where it was there associated with the sun god Horus, and it is therefore interesting to consider the ship as a kind of sun disc turned over onto its side and flying horizontally through space. It is reminiscent of the giant eagle that carries the hero Vainamoinen on its back in the Finnish epic known as *The Kalevala*[36] from whence Tolkien borrowed his race of giant eagles for *The Hobbit*.

Thus, nearing the film's halfway mark, we have been presented with a series of characters all trapped inside various prisons and situations of confinement: the capture, first of Princess Leia by the Empire; then the jettison of the droids and their capture on the surface of Tatooine by the Jawas who then sell them into slavery to the family of a boy who perceives his life as a kind of prison in which he is confined to the drudgery of farm work that he doesn't really want to do and wasn't cut out for. R2D2, as we have seen, was the first to make his escape as he traced a line of flight that led Luke to the house of Ben Kenobi, thereby saving his life, for while he was away from his home Luke's family was massacred by Imperial stormtroopers searching for the droids. But that had the effect of cutting him loose from his confinement to the life of a farmer and thus enabled him to begin his ascent from the pit of the earth to his arrival along with Ben and the droids at Mos Eisley spaceport where the viewer encountered yet another character, Han Solo, confined to yet another prison, in this case, one of economic indebtedness.

Thus, when the ship breaks free of the gravitational pull of the lower elements—personified nicely by Jabba the Hut—into outer space, Luke is finally carried once and for all upwards from the planet and outwards into the realm of Spirit, with all its masculine technological constructions. He is on the way to liberate Princess Leia from *her* prison inside the megamachine personified by the Death Star, carried on the back of a flying Garuda bird whose semiotics have been recoded to fit the sign regime of space opera science fiction.

SECOND HALF:
AGAINST THE
DEATH STAR

The Destruction of Alderaan

(57:01 – 59:35)

The film's second half opens, appropriately enough, with a shot of the Death Star drifting like a rogue planet through space on its way to Princess Leia's home planet of Alderaan, which is a blue and white disc in the distance that looks similar to earth.

Whereas the first half of the film had been concerned with the desert planet of Tatooine and the attempts of a "tetramorphic Subject" to escape from its various situations of confinement, the second half involves the battle of the protagonists against another planetary orb, the Death Star. The two halves of the film thus concern two orbs, one, Tatooine--essentially inspired by Frank Herbert's desert planet of Arrakis in his *Dune* novels--the other, the Death Star--inspired by Asimov's city-wide-planet of Trantor in his *Foundation* novels. Hence, the formula structuring the entire narrative of Episode 4 is to pit Arrakis against Trantor: mud-brown earth tones against steel and gunmetal gray. The creatures of mud and earth—on the political plane, Fanon's "Wretched of the Earth"-- against those of a hi-tech world-city-as-cosmopolis.

Tatooine is a difficult planet to live on: it is a place full of traps for the unwary—gangsters like Jabba the Hut, for instance, or attacks from the Sandpeople--whereas the Death Star *is* a prison, and one that is armed for the destruction of entire planets. It is a world-swallowing machine, just like the American Empire of today.

In the present scene, another interior shot inside the Death Star shows Princess Leia being escorted down a hallway into the main control room of the space station, where Tarkin and Darth Vader are waiting for her. Tarkin threatens to use the full operational force of the Death Star—for its inaugural planetary destruction—on her home planet of Alderaan unless she gives them the location of the rebels' secret fortress. Leia, under stress, lies and tells him that the rebels are on the planet of Dantooine, but Tarkin goes ahead with the act of destruction anyway, accusing her of being "far too trusting." A shot of green rays gathering to form a single mighty pulse is shown emanating from the power disc of the Death Star, which fires at Alderaan and destroys it completely in a white hot flash.

Meanwhile, a shot aboard the *Millenium Falcon* shows Luke using his father's lightsaber against a small round orb known as a "training remote" (in a way, it is a miniature version of the Death Star that he is about to go up against). Ben suddenly collapses, however, to a nearby seat and Luke shuts off his lightsaber to assist him, asking him what's wrong. Ben explains to him that he just felt a great disturbance of agony within the Force, as though a thousand souls had just cried out in pain.

As I remarked above, the film's two halves are structured on the basic binarity of the planet of Tatooine and the mechanized and artificial "planet" of the Death Star. This tension between the two orbs is the difference engine that drives the energy of the narrative forward. Tatooine is brown and copper, the colors of the dirt of the earth itself, whereas

104

the colors of the Death Star are a cold cloudy-day gray, the color of a handgun, say, or some other device for shooting ballistic missiles. It is a semiotic opposition of earth against the global Anti-world of communications satellites, drones and electromagnetic pulse fields that surround the entire planet within a technoskeleton.

But the binarity, as Derrida would say, is actually a false one, since the earth is actually contained *inside* the Death Star, since the Death Star signifies its satellization and transformation into a planet that is literally capable of blowing up other planets. But just as the Death Star destroys worlds, such as Alderaan, so too, the globalization of the earth by the Western Empire erases and effaces the local, the particular and boundaries of all kinds. It has destroyed the "world" of the Native Americans; it has destroyed and colonized huge parts of Africa; and it is currently attempting, this Death Star, to force the Islamic sign regime to fit into and conform to its own codings. It is a technoskeleton that destroys other worlds by erasing the significances of their meanings as particular *places*. Just as Alain Badiou pointed out in his critique of globalization in his book *Ethics*, other cultures are only "tolerated" in the name of "multi-culturalism" insofar as they remain like *us*: that is to say, respect Human Rights, Free Trade Agreements and adopt democracy and capitalism. Any forms of cultural otherness which are *too* Other—such as female clitoredectomies; or the wearing of burkas; or giving women lower status—are not respected and in fact, are regarded as barbaric.[37] You and your state apparatus are only given loans from the IMF and the World Bank to the degree that your culture is willing to adopt capitalism and democracy, whether these structures are consistent with the cultural traditions of your local society or not. Otherness is thereby in process of being effaced from the local as the global ecumene of Anti-World makes every place the same as every other place. Heidegger was the first to warn of the cultural nihilism that would result from such technological enframing.

Also note that Tarkin's order to destroy Alderaan is a mechanized and artificial version of the ancient mythical Left Hand of God, which destroys and wipes out entire worlds, including God's own creation itself with the Great Flood. The cities of Sodom and Gomorrah, for instance, are destroyed—together with every inhabitant within them— for their wicked ways, but Tarkin destroys Alderaan simply as a demonstration to Princess Leia of the full might of the Empire that they are now rebelling against. In other words, what used to be ancient myth is now entering into the Real as a result of technological "progress." Whole worlds, entire planets and moons, even, can now be destroyed by the human appropriation of Acts of God simply by using nuclear weapons. Hiroshima was the structural equivalent to the destruction of Alderaan, for both were primarily demonstrations to the rest of the world of the newly operational might and power of the Empire. Nagasaki was also destroyed not so much because it was necessary—it wasn't, for the Japanese were already in process of working out the terms of their surrender—but for purposes of mere symmetry, because unconsciously it formed a modern equivalent of the destructions of the pair of cities in the Bible called Sodom and Gomorrah. Biblical myth is so engrained in the Western mentality that it lurks beneath everything the West does, quietly structuring what it effectuates into the Real as mythic DNA programming for the unfolding of events in the physical world.

The destruction of Hiroshima and Nagasaki as real world echoes of Sodom and Gomorrah was a way of saying to the enemies of Empire, "*We* are God now, since we have appropriated all of His powers. Resistance to the sign regime[38] and overcodings of Empire is useless." So too, Tarkin's destruction of Alderaan is merely an echo of this historical event which is folded up like an embryo inside of it.

108

Luke's First Training Lesson

(59:36 – 1:02:30)

Ben now tells Luke that he ought to resume his lesson, and so he turns his lightsaber back on as he goes to work in combat against the training remote (a scene derived, perhaps, from the training of Paul Atreides in Frank Herbert's first *Dune* novel). Han Solo then comes down the hallway reassuring everyone that they have outrun the imperial starships, but as nobody pays him any attention—Ben is brooding on the disturbance he has just felt in the Force, while Luke is training—he says, with some sarcasm, "Don't everybody thank me all at once." He then tells them that they should arrive at Alderaan in 0200 hours.

R2D2 and Chewbacca are engaged, meanwhile, in another sort of agon as the two play a kind of holographic chess game with three-dimensional stop-motion animation figures. R2's little creature makes a move that defeats one of Chewbacca's, who protests, while C3P0, sitting between them insists that it was a fair move. Han Solo advises that it is unwise to upset a Wookie, and when C3P0 points out with some rationality that nobody worries about upsetting a droid, Solo points out that droids don't pull the arms out of people's sockets when they lose, whereas Wookies have been known to do that. C3P0 advises R2, in light of this, to let the Wookie win.

The scene is small and apparently insignificant, but it pits the mammalian brain—the limbic ring with all its emotional responses—against the ratiocinative intellect, which simply proceeds through the world by means of making calculations. The mammalian brain is much older, more irrational and embedded *deep* in the core of the architecture of the human brain. Passion, love, suffering and anger come out of it, and rationality does not appeal to it at all or appease it; Violence as a problem-solving strategy is therefore always—and will always be—a distinct possibility for it.

Luke, meanwhile, is wrestling with the training remote, which blasts him, to the amusement of Han Solo, who insists that outdated religions and archaic weapons are no match for a good blaster at one's side. Luke turns off the lightsaber and insists, accusingly, that Han Solo does not believe in the Force, to which Solo replies that he has been from one end of the galaxy to another and seen no evidence of any mystical energy field controlling *his* destiny.

Ben now decides to make the lesson a bit harder and gives Luke a helmet to wear, with the blast shield pulled down. Luke asks how he can possibly fight the remote with the blast shield pulled down, but Ben tells him to act on his instincts. When Luke asks if the Force controls his actions, Ben tells him that it only partially does so, but that it also obeys your commands.

Luke then reignites his lightsaber as the training remote hovers and spins in the air in front of him, zapping him once again, much to Han Solo's amusement. Ben insists, though, that he needs to stretch out with his feelings. Luke tries again, and this time he manages to block three blasts from the remote with a skillful swing of his lightsaber.

Luke takes the helmet off and says that it seemed like he *could* almost feel something there, but Han Solo says he calls it "luck." Kenobi insists that, in his experience, there is no such thing as luck. Solo then notices that they are approaching the location of Alderaan.

The scene is actually a philosophical discussion in the guise of mass entertainment. Solo's stance—consistent with his name—is that his will is free and he is an entity that is under no obligations to any sort of Higher Self or mystical energy field. He is, in other words, in that mode of self-sufficiency which Heidegger termed *Vorhandenheit,* and which was a construction of the metaphysical age that began with Socrates and Plato and then began, once again, with Descartes. The self in such a mode exists completely independently of all other forces, entities, angels, beings or gods, and such an idea is what led to the Western philosophical construction of the Transcendental Subject, as Kant called it.[39] The Western subject, in the metaphysical age's understanding of Being, is a pure subject beholding pure objects. Both subject and object are deworlded—that is to say, denuded of any worldly qualities--to which Heidegger responded by taking the Subject and re-embedding him back into the concrete physical world as *Dasein,* which means in essence, "self *plus* a particular world that one is always already engaged in performing tasks in."[40]

But the Force is actually a much older idea: it is a uteromorphic structure, a web-like all-encompassing field of energy with a point-like unity to it which the Swiss philosopher Jean Gebser called "the magical consciousness structure," which is a sort of invisible spider web surrounding the realm of physical matter and which composed of etheric filaments of energy that vibrate at certain higher frequencies—and which therefore cannot be seen with the naked eye, for physical matter vibrates at low, slow densities. Solo is articulating what Gebser called "the rational

111

consciousness structure," which is, more or less, the same thing as Heidegger's metaphysical age from Plato to Husserl in which *Vorhandenheit* reigned as the main understanding of Being, a vision in which the self is thought of as a lone self-sufficient entity with free will that is in dialogue with no outer entities, since those very outer entities—angels, spirits, etc.—were anathematized by that structure so that it could develop a world view based entirely upon freedom of the will.

The lightsaber is not so much a simple tactical weapon like a sword, but something closer to a dowsing rod that senses particularly complex condensations of energy that resonate through the web of the Force. The Jedi knight is able to channel those energies through the lightsaber itself, but it can also encounter hostility or aggression in the form of extremely low vibrations that create dense pockets within the Force which function as a resistance to be overcome by means of the lightsaber's channeling of higher frequency energy, which is why material objects, in the later *Star Wars* films, simply melt away in its path. It isn't the lightsaber that cuts things to pieces, but rather the lightsaber as an extension of the will of the Jedi knight, who uses it to channel energy from the Force to specific points of resistance in its uteromorphic energy field.

The entire cosmos, in *Star Wars*, is contained within a uteromorphic structure, for the Force is made of etheric energy patterns which it is the task of the Jedi knight to study and learn to manipulate, just the way a scientist, by analogy, learns to manipulate physical matter by studying the mathematical equations that unlock its potentialities.

Thus, when Luke successfully blocks the training remote's blasts, it is an equivalent moment to the scene at the climax in which he destroys the Death Star only when he turns off his navi-computer and uses his intuition. The training remote is a kind of miniature Death Star, and his agon with it in this scene, is already preparing us for his encounter with the technological monstrosity known as the Death Star, which has used masculine machine-age metaphysics to capture and appropriate female curvilinearity.

Captured by the Death Star
(1:02:31 – 1:10:12)

Han Solo indicates that their ship is now approaching Alderaan and so he gets up and heads for the pilot seat. Luke tells Ben on the way that he thought he *could* almost feel something for a fleeting moment during the training session, and Ben informs him that he's just taken his first step into a larger world.

Next comes a scene set inside the conference room inside the Death Star, in which Tarkin and Vader are busy on some project when an administrative official interrupts and tells them that they have conducted a search on the planet of Dantooine and found only the long deserted remains of a rebel base but not an active one. Tarkin is furious that Leia has lied to them, but Vader is nonplussed.

The *Millenium Falcon*, meanwhile, comes out of hyperspace into an asteroid field. It is apparently all that is left of the disintegrated planet of Alderaan. Ben, sitting behind Solo in the pilot's seat, says that he knows very well the planet has been destroyed, but Solo insists that such a feat would be a technological impossibility. A lone Imperial T.I.E. Fighter races past them, and Ben wonders what such a short range craft would be doing on its own in deep space. Solo decides to follow it and shoot it down in case it may have identified the *Falcon*. Ben insists on letting it go, but

Luke points out that the ship appears to be heading for a small, pale moon that is rapidly approaching their vector. As Solo prepares to shoot down the fighter, however, Ben tells them that what they're looking at is not a moon but rather *a space station*. Solo is incredulous. Luke says he has a bad feeling about all this and it doesn't take Solo very long to agree with him: he tells Chewie to reverse the ship, but it is too late, for it has gotten caught in a tractor beam which locks onto it and pulls it steadily in toward the Death Star.

The *Falcon* is pulled as though by a magnet into a polished steel docking bay with gleaming black floors, where it lands softly, while Imperial stormtroopers are scrambled in lines to prepare for boarding it. Tarkin, still in the conference room, receives word that the ship has been identified as the same one which escaped from Mos Eisley Spaceport. Vader, standing across from him, tells him that the droids must be trying to return the stolen plans to the princess and that she may still be of some use to them.

When Vader arrives, breathing raggedly, in the docking bay, an official is just coming out of the *Falcon* and informs him that it has been abandoned and must be a decoy of some sort, since the ship's log indicates that its crew jettisoned from it sometime after take-off and several escape pods are missing. Vader, however, is suspicious: he senses a disturbance in the Force, an old presence with a shadowy aura that he has not felt in many years. He pauses moodily a moment, then walks away, after ordering that the ship be checked more thoroughly.

Inside the ship, a group of stormtroopers are clearing out, believing it to be empty, but the floor panels suddenly pop up to reveal Han, Luke, Ben and Chewbacca in hiding (once again reiterating the narrative's vectors, namely, that they have come *up* to the Death Star *from below* riding on

116

the back of a huge mechanized falcon). Luke says it's a good thing Han had these secret compartments and Han says that though he'd used them in the past for smuggling, he never thought he'd be smuggling himself. He points out that even if they could get past the security forces, they'd never get loose from the tractor beam, but Ben insists that that particular task be left up to him. Solo calls him a fool, and in response, Ben asks, rhetorically, who is the more foolish: the fool or the one who follows the fool? (This scene is borrowed from Kurosawa's sequel to *Yojimbo*, in a film called *Sanjuro*).[41]

A special scanning crew of two men arrives to conduct a more thorough investigation and they go up the ship's ramp, carrying heavy equipment between them. Two stormtroopers are standing guard at the entrance ramp, but when they hear a voice from inside the ship yell down at them to come up and give the scanning crew a hand, they go up the ramp and after a pause, the sound of a blaster is heard going off twice.

Inside the docking bay's control room, meanwhile, the official in charge notices that the stormtroopers assigned to guard the ship's entrance ramp are not present, and when he attempts to contact one of them, he then looks out the window over the bay to see one of them come walking down out of the ship, shaking his helmet. The official then tells his partner that one of the guards has a bad transmitter and that he must go investigate, but when he opens the door to the control room he is taken by surprise as Chewbacca erupts at him across the threshold, tossing him aside, while Han, dressed as a stormtrooper, blasts his way in and shoots the other technician.

Luke, also dressed as a stormtrooper, comes in behind him, closing the door and removing his helmet, complaining that Chewbacca and Han are making too much noise. Han tells him he'd prefer a straight fight to sneaking around.

C3P0 then informs Ben Kenobi that he and R2D2 have found the imperial outlet and Kenobi directs R2 to plug into it, since he should be able to interpret the entire imperial network. As R2 scans the system, his information informs them that there are seven power stations that control the tractor beam and that if any one of them is damaged, then that would be sufficient to allow the ship to leave. Kenobi decides to undertake the task alone—for he also has another agenda--and tells the others that he doesn't think they can help him and insists on going alone. Solo doesn't object, but Luke has separation anxiety and wants to go with him. Ben, however, tells him that his path lies along a different destiny than Luke's. He tells him that the Force will always be with him, then disappears into the depths of the Death Star on his lonely mission.

Note, once again, the narrative's vectors: the fourfold Subject composed of Han, Luke, Chewie and Ben have come *up* from the Underworld of Tatooine via the Falcon, and entered into the depths of another orb, an artificial one, in this case, that is essentially a cosmopolis in disguise. They have moved from the local to the global and the international. It is as though a farmer from a small village in North Africa had migrated to a cosmopolis of steel and glass like Dubai and entered into another world altogether, one that is composed of steel framed technologies welded together with electronics to create a global mesh of electromagnetic pulse signals that have captured and imprisoned the planet within it. In the metaphoric language of science fiction, it *appears* as though the protagonists have flown via spaceship from one planet to another (artificial) one, but the semiotics of the narrative connote the shift from the particular and unique *place*—village, hamlet, farm, etc.—to entry inside the world-as-global-cosmopolis which the Death Star represents.

The Death Star erases all places from the maps: it simply deletes them in the metaphoric act of blowing up planets, but in reality it is overcoding and homogenizing such places so that they conform to the sign regime of Cosmopolis.

The Death Star is the steel and glass urb-as-orb of the highly artificial world city that instantly provincializes all other places on the map, even cultural towns and small cities of the world of Old Europe like Venice and Cologne. Its sole purpose is exactly as Lucas has pictured it for us: it is destructive, for it is about erasing local cultures and overcoding them with the International Style of Modernity, together with all its Non-Places, airports, parking lots, strip malls, gas stations, etc. It sucks in flows of every kind—people, migrants, ships, anyone and anything in the dromosphere, uprooted peasants looking for work or soldiers who have returned from battle to find their homesteads ruined—and codes them so that they flow through the striated spaces of its modular and angular topology.[42] (From a distance, the Death Star appears to be round like a planet, but when one gets up close, as for instance during the film's climactic battle sequence, all the buildings are angular: not a curvilinear structure in sight).

So we have gone from one world to another in an ascent that is also positioning two of the film's main characters at poles apart: note that the sequence carefully begins to align Ben Kenobi against Darth Vader, like north and south magnetic poles aligning along the narrative curvature to opposite points. For if Ben Kenobi represents the old world of art and culture of the Jedi—the samurai, let's say, *before* Japan's Meiji Restoration put him out of business and made his practice illegal while the Japanese state began to industrialize along Western models—then Darth Vader is the *Anti*-Jedi in just the same way that the Death Star is an Anti-World. He is a former Jedi knight who has been *swallowed up* by the International Modernity of the Death Star, just as it has captured Princess Leia as goddess of the earth in modern guise.

The tetramorphic Subject composed of Han, Luke, Ben and Chewbacca is about to get a morphological restructuring, for Ben now *drops out* of the fourfold as he disappears into the techno-labyrinth of the Death Star, while Princess Leia will *surface* from out of its depths in order to take over his semiotic slot as part of the newly structured fourfold. Ben will then form a binarity as a completely separate structure, as he becomes the polar opposite of Darth Vader, with whom he is about to settle an old score. Once he has "lost" the fight against Darth Vader, *his* semiotic vacancy as the polar opposite of Vader will be replaced in *The Empire Strikes Back* by Luke Skywalker, who himself will drop away from the tetramorphic Subject as he is replaced by C3P0, his annoying rational twin. In *Return of the Jedi*, the fourfold will be composed of Han, Leia, Chewbacca and C3P0, as the binarity formed by Darth Vader against Luke Skywalker— together with his mechanized "animal" companion R2D2— separates off into a parallel narrative.

The Rescue of Princess Leia
(1:10:13 – 1:17:13)

After Ben's departure, Han and Luke get into an argument regarding how much "trouble" Ben has gotten them into, when they are interrupted by the excited electronic beeps of R2D2, who tells C3P0 that he has located Princess Leia (note that just as only C3P0 can understand the electronic beeps of R2D2's language, so Han Solo is the only one who can understand the howls and grunts of Chewbacca). When Luke insists that they must rescue the princess, Solo sits down and decides that he has already gotten himself into enough trouble as it is and has no interest in rescuing any princess, whether she is scheduled to be "terminated" or not. But when Luke highlights how wealthy she must be, Han perks up, and when Luke assures him that a tremendous reward would be granted to anyone who rescued her, he decides to go along with Luke's plan.

They then put Chewbacca in handcuffs and pretend that he is their prisoner as they escort him, helmets back on, down the bluish-gray metallic corridors of the Death Star leading to the detention area.

Meanwhile, Ben Kenobi is shown lurking in the shadows as he makes his way behind contingents of marching stormtroopers in the gloomy hallways. There is a shot of Darth Vader walking alone, who stops for a moment, sensing little tremors and seismic shakes in the Force as the result of proximity to Kenobi, then moves on.

When Solo and Luke have arrived at the detention center with Chewbacca between them, the guard asks them where they are taking their prisoner, and Han and Luke insist that he is a prisoner transfer from Cell Block 1138. The guard says that he hasn't been notified of any such transfer and as he attempts to communicate with his superiors, Chewbacca breaks loose as Solo hands a rifle over to him and all three begin shooting wildly at the guards and the cameras until they have taken control over the detention center.

Solo then finds out what cell block the princess is in and tells Luke to go and get her while he takes off his helmet and attempts to forestall the security forces that then try to communicate with him via com-link. He ends up blasting the link and yelling at Luke to hurry up for they are about to have company.

Luke locates the cell and hits the button that causes the door to slide upwards. The princess is lying inside her hard, angular cell with no cushions or curvilinearity of any kind, attempting to sleep when Luke erupts into the cell and tells her that his name is Luke Skywalker and that he has brought her droids and Ben Kenobi along with him to rescue her. At the sound of Ben Kenobi's name, she wakes up fast and joins Luke as they race out of the cell and into the detention center's hallway.

Vader, meanwhile, enters Tarkin's conference room to inform him that Obi-Wan Kenobi is alive and well and hiding somewhere on the Death Star. When Tarkin doubts him and insists that Vader is all that is left of the Jedi order, Vader tells him not to underestimate the power of the Force.

A voice comes over the intercom to inform Tarkin that there is an emergency in the detention center, and when Tarkin asks whether it has to do with the princess's cell, he receives confirmation. Vader tells him that Obi-Wan is most definitely aboard the Death Star and when Tarkin tells him that he must not be allowed to escape, Vader insists that escape is not his plan and that he must face him alone.

The princess, then, is the Muse of Western Civilization, a signifier whose career began as the Virgin Mary, who was the primary inspiration for the building of civilization in the days of chivalry, knights and captive princesses held up in castles and in the building of cathedrals as uteromorphic vessels within which to contain and overcode all other signifiers. But as Henry Adams, in his piece on "The Dynamo and the Virgin," back at the turn of the twentieth century in 1907 pointed out, the Virgin was engulfed by the Machine—metonymically personified, for Adams, by the electric dynamo—which displaced her to become the motivating force for the construction of industrial, rather than Western Christian, civilization.[43]

Star Wars, then, attempts to *reverse* the swallowing up of the princess by the machine, by *extracting* her from the machine and pulling her back into the gravitational orbit of the earth itself as a Gaian system capable of self-regulation and homeostasis. If the Death Star as part for the whole stands for the Empire, then the Empire is the ultimate technoskeleton that has come to surround and overcode the earth with artificial, rather than, natural codes. It is attempting to replace all of Gaia's own codes with codes that have sprung, like Athena from the head of Zeus, from the paternal order of Father Science.

But we are currently seeing today the result of building a technical exoskeleton around the earth, for Gaia has her own codes and operates on her own sign regime in the form of the bacterial immune system of the earth that has created the architecture of the atmosphere and released all of its oxygen as a by-product of photosynthesis that has colored the sky blue. (Blue, recall, being one of the Virgin's primary colors). To the army of cloned stormtroopers in *Star Wars*, there corresponds the army of bacteria at the disposal of the earth and its homeostatic systems that are currently resisting the industrial overcoding with monster hurricanes, record heat waves, record droughts and epic tornadoes. The Age of Catastrophe, as I have written in my book about the subject, is the Gaian response to Henry Adams's Industrial Age.[44]

In *Star Wars*, the princess is like a chess piece: whichever side possesses her, be it Empire or Rebellion, is the side that is going to win the battle, for she is the primary Muse that inspires the whole operation.

Is it going to be the ancient Paleolithic Great Mother with no face and huge milk-giving breasts—which later becomes the many-breasted Diana of Ephesus—or Athena, the mind-born and state sponsored patroness of scientists, technicians and soldiers?

Trash Compactor

(1:17:14 – 1:25:00)

In this scene, Han, Luke, Princess Leia and Chewbacca are cornered by stormtroopers in the detention center's hallway. A gunfight is going on, with pink laser blasts flying back and forth as the four protagonists try to assess their situation. Luke asks C3P0 on his com-link if there is any other way out, but 3P0 tells him that all systems have been alerted to their presence and there is no way out but the way they entered. Leia barks insultingly at Solo, asking why they attempted a rescue with no escape plan, and Solo yells back at her from across the hallway that Luke is the brains of the operation. Leia then takes charge and grabs a blaster, fires once down the hallway and then shoots a hole into the wall and jumps down into a garbage chute. Han kicks a reluctant Chewbacca in after her, and then both he and Luke follow.

The four then find themselves inside one of the Death Star's garbage chutes: chunks of discarded, twisted metal and rusted pieces of steel and other effluvia surround them. The walls are metal, brown and stained. Solo attempts to fire his weapon at what appears to be a door (in reality, it is the pressure maintenance hatch through which they will ultimately escape), but the laser bolt ricochets like a bullet and nearly kills them. Luke says he has already tried that and the four stand silent a moment, listening: something is alive and swimming around in the chute with them. At one point, a single reptilian eye on an alien stalk pops up and looks around like a periscope, then disappears. In another moment, it grabs Luke with a long tentacle that wraps around him and pulls him under the brackish, coppery water. He surfaces with the tentacle wrapped around him and yells at Solo to blast it, which he does, but the creature drags him beneath the surface and for a few moments, it appears as though it has made off with him. There is a metallic sound that echoes around them, and then Luke resurfaces telling them that the creature just let him go and disappeared. (The scene is a foreshadowing of Luke's descent into the Underworld of Dagobah in *The Empire Strikes Back*).

There is another ominous pause, and then a factory-like grinding of metal begins to cause the walls to move in on them, slowly compacting the garbage. While Leia and Solo try to brace the two walls by raising a long silvery metal pole, Luke yells into his com-link at 3PO but there is no answer. The droids, meanwhile, have been detained: they have locked themselves in a closet, and when stormtroopers enter, they pretend that they were held captive by the rebels and 3PO tells them that if they hurry, the stormtroopers might catch them on their way to the prison level. The stormtroopers then leave, but one of them stays behind to guard the area. C3PO tells him that his companion's circuits have been overloaded with all this excitement and that he would like to take him down to the maintenance level. The stormtrooper grants him permission.

3PO tells R2 to plug in to the Death Star's main computer and find out if their companions have been captured. R2 does so, but he also reminds 3PO to turn his com-link back on and when he does, he hears Luke shouting at him to shut up and tell R2 to shut down all the garbage chutes on the detention level. 3P0, in a panic, tells R2 to shut down *all* the garbage mashers and as he does this, the walls stop and the four protagonists begin yelling with joy, although 3P0, always the inveterate pessimist, thinks they're being crushed to death. Luke reassures him they're still alive and to get R2 to open the pressure maintenance hatch in their particular garbage chute.

Recall that all four protagonists, as the viewer has encountered them one by one, has each been confined to one or another prison: Luke on his farm, Solo and Chewbacca indebted to Jabba the Hut, and Leia as a literal prisoner in her cell inside the Death Star. But in this scene, all four protagonists now find themselves in the *same* situation of confinement, as the garbage masher prepares to grind them up. They have been tossed onto the Empire's midden heap of discarded signifiers,[45] for the Empire simply grinds those signifiers that it finds it cannot overcode with its own sign regime into pieces. The four have found themselves in the digestive belly of the Death Star, which proceeds to grind them up with its own metallic enzymes since it no longer has any use for them. The monster in the chute with them is simply a left-over signifier from the mythical age, like one of the monsters fought by a Hercules or a Jason during their exploits. The Empire, with its global codes, is in the process of dissolving all signifiers remaining from previous ages--in Peter Sloterdijk's terminology, the metaphysical and pre-metaphysical ages (or, in Gebser's, the magical and mythical consciousness structures). Just as the Western intellect which produces the machines did so by grinding down the dragons, myths, witches and monsters of the Medieval order—which Bosch captures in the entirety of his artwork as a sort of gigantic midden heap of discarded signifiers left over from the prior Medieval age of monsters—so the Empire is busy grinding down all local codes, myths, rituals and religions which have functioned to impart the local with meaning and signification.

But there is also another level to the scene, for it is analogous to the ancient archaeometallurgical practice known as "cupellation," in which a particular metal—silver or gold, let's say—was extracted from its ore by carefully putting it into a mould that was then placed with tongs into a furnace. When the tongs were used to pull the mould out of the furnace, the result was liquid metal that had taken on the shape of the mould and could be extracted from it, once the liquid cooled, in the shape of a single ingot.

Recall that Ben Kenobi had departed from the tetramorphic Subject comprised originally by him and Han, Luke and Chewbacca. He was replaced by Leia, however, and now the four are placed inside something that is analogous to a furnace, where they are crushed together to form the new ingot that is equivalent to an entirely new tetramorphic Subject formed by the quaternion of Princess Leia, Han Solo, Luke Skywalker and Chewbacca. Just as Han—the extravert—should be drawn in a kind of diagram directly across from the introverted Luke, so Princess Leia should be drawn in opposition to Chewbacca, for her earthly semiotics tie her in with the animals of the earth, and especially its mammalian animals (this is further developed in *Return of the Jedi* with the instant rapport that she forms with the Ewoks).

Thus, when the compacting has, as it were been completed, what emerges is the ingot of a newly formed tetramorphic Subject of three males and one female (or, conversely, three humans and one animal).

The Escape from the Death Star
(1:25:01 – 1:33:15)

A shot now follows of Ben Kenobi, lightsaber in hand (though inactive), as he sneaks down a gray and blue metallic hallway and creeps into one of the Death Star's power stations. He steps out onto the ledge surrounding the pylon, around which there drops a chasm leading deep into the abyss of the Death Star, and begins to turn off a series of switches that will deactivate the tractor beam keeping the *Millenium Falcon* hostage in the docking bay.

The scene then shifts to an area outside the maintenance hatch of the garbage chute, where the four protagonists are cleaning themselves off. Solo insists that as long as they avoid any more "female advice," as he puts it, then they should do just fine. Leia, however, tells him firmly that she has no idea who he is, and doesn't care, but that from now on, he is to take orders only from her. Solo insists that *he* only takes orders from himself, and Leia counters by wondering how he's managed to stay alive so long.

Meanwhile, a group of stormtroopers shows up near the power station where Kenobi is still deactivating the tractor beam. The group marches away, leaving behind a pair of stormtroopers to stand guard, who hold casual conversation while Kenobi slips past them, using the Force to momentarily distract their attention while he disappears into the shadows.

The scene then returns to the four protagonists who look out through a window over the docking bay, where the *Millenium Falcon* is being guarded by stormtroopers. Leia turns to Solo and remarks that if he came to rescue her in that thing, then he must be braver than she thought. Luke turns on his com-link to find C3P0, who tells him that he and R2 are waiting in a hangar below them. Luke tells him they'll be down shortly, but as they cross into the hallway, they encounter a group of stormtroopers who begin firing at them. Solo fires back and then chases them down the hallway, yelling for the rest of them to get to the ship. Impressed, Leia then remarks on his courage.

Luke and Leia then head the other way, pursued by stormtroopers, until they come to a stop at the edge of a deactivated bridge that leaves a huge chasm yawning beneath them. Stormtroopers are firing at their backs, so Leia hits the button that closes the door behind them, but there is no way to lock the door. Luke then blasts the control panel to jam the door shut, but it is also the same panel that would've extended the bridge, so, as stormtroopers fire down on them from a level above, he throws a grappling hook up around a fixture and Leia kisses him for good luck as they swing together across the chasm to the other transom.

A group of stormtroopers is now shown marching rapidly down a hallway past Ben Kenobi, who waits for a moment in the shadows before proceeding down a darkened corridor, lightsaber drawn but not yet activated.

Solo and Chewbacca are then shown running from stormtroopers in pursuit, and they manage to hop through a set of closing blast doors that cut them off from the stormtroopers.

Kenobi, meanwhile, wearing his hood above his head,

enters a shadowy corridor where he finds Darth Vader waiting for him, lightsaber drawn and glowing a hot, incandescent red in the half-gloom. He tells Kenobi that he's been waiting for him while Kenobi ignites his own lightsaber, which illuminates blue-hot in the dark. Vader tells him that when last he saw him he was still but a learner, but that now *he* is the master. Kenobi tells him he is merely a master of evil as they cross glowing, humming lightsabers that send shattering green sparks of light flickering everywhere. Their movements are slow and awkward, for they are both old, aged masters who have long since passed their prime, and Vader tells Kenobi that his powers are weak. Kenobi counters by saying that he can't win, because if Vader strikes him down then Kenobi will become even more powerful than ever.

On the ground floor of the docking bay, meanwhile, the four protagonists are reunited near the ship, but it is still guarded by a cluster of stormtroopers. Solo tells them he hopes Kenobi got that tractor beam out of commission or they won't be able to leave.

Across the bay, Vader and Kenobi then surface into view, framed by the rectangle of an open blast door, clashing their sparking, popping lightsabers, which distracts the attention of the stormtroopers guarding the ship, who now run across to watch the spectacle.

C3P0, from his position in the hangar on the other side of the ship, sees them leave and tells R2 that it's time for them to go. The other four protagonists likewise see their chance and begin to make for the ship, but when Luke sees Kenobi fighting Darth Vader, he stops. Ben notices that Luke sees him, smiles to himself, and then raises his lightsaber directly before him, unresisting as Vader strikes at him and his body dematerializes, leaving behind only an empty brown robe that Vader checks with his boot.

Luke yells out for Ben, traumatized by his sudden disappearance, but it is too late and the other three run up the ramp into the ship as the stormtroopers spot them and begin shooting from across the bay. Luke remains a moment, firing at the stormtroopers, until he hears the voice of Ben inside his head telling him to flee.

Solo and Chewbacca are then shown strapping into their pilot seats and Solo reiterates his hope that Kenobi got the tractor beam out of commission. He tells Chewbacca to "hit it," and the dingy, off-white colored ship lifts from the glossy black floor of the bay, turns around 180 degrees, and blasts off into outer space.

Thus, the *Millenium Falcon* is the mechanical bird which has carried the protagonists away now from *two* orbs: the first being Tatooine—a signifier representing earth itself—the second being an artificial orb, that of the Death Star, a mechanized labyrinth. The second escape differs from the first, however, in that they have successfully managed to extract the Muse—Princess Leia—from her prison inside the mechanical fortress, at the cost, however, of trading her out for Ben Kenobi, whom they have (seemingly) left behind. Like Jason fleeing with Medea from the fortress of King Aeetes—which turned out to have been a mistake on his part—or Theseus taking Ariadne, the daughter of King Minos, with him from the labyrinth, this whole sequence has probably the most mythic feel about it of the entire film.

With the princess safely in their care now, they may return with her to the rebel base, which is located on a forest planet that is also a signifier for the earth itself, from whence they may study the architectural plans of the Death Star to learn of its Achilles Heel, like the one missing scale of the dragon Smaug in *The Hobbit*, the only vulnerable part on his body that would enable one to slay him.

Kenobi has fallen away into the Underworld of the Force, but this has the magical effect of transforming him into something more like an electromagnetic field: he is now simultaneously everywhere and nowhere at once. Luke has, in a sense, interiorized him, or introjected him into the *inside* of his mind—analogous to the labyrinth of the Death Star in terms of its many folds—where he serves as the function of Luke's conscience from here on out.

So whereas Kenobi, as a part of the original tetramorphic subject of the film, has gone *inside* into concealment, Princess Leia has been extracted and taken *outside* into unconcealment, where she can now function as the Muse inspiring the entire Rebellion against the Empire. Kenobi now functions as the personal conscience for Luke, whereas Leia is the collective anima of the entire operation who advises and gives commands to the rebels on how to defeat the Empire. This algebraic function, as it were, of crossing out Ben Kenobi and extracting Leia to the other side of the equation has given the Rebel forces the advantage which they so badly needed, for now they have *two* mythic figures to aid them in fighting the dragon of the Empire, the Wise Old Man and the Anima who animates the spheres and planets and knows the mechanics of their dynamism. This equation was essential for them to beat the Death Star, for without the Princess and her knowledge of its labyrinthine interiority, they could never have defeated it. She is equivalent to Ariadne in this sense, for she brings with her an intimate knowledge of the interior lay-out of the Death Star as labyrinth.

The lightsaber duel between Ben Kenobi and Darth Vader, moreover, was also symmetric in that, as we later learn in *Revenge of the Sith*, Kenobi had beaten Vader and left him for dead at the edge of a pool of volcanic lava. He was only saved by the intervention of the Emperor, who arrived just in time to preserve and transform him into a biomechanical centaur.

However, there is a hidden astronomical dimension to their encounter aboard the Death Star, in which Vader thinks he is victorious this time round, for there is a gap of exactly 19 years between their two encounters (according to *Star Wars* lore). The 19 year cycle was known to the ancients as a Metonic Cycle, which is a coincidence of the lunar and solar calendars. Nineteen revolutions of the earth around the sun corresponds to 235 synodic months at which time, the sun and the moon are, as it were, reunited against the background of the fixed stars. Hence, in *The Odyssey*, it takes Odysseus—the solar hero--precisely nineteen years to be reunited with Penelope—a lunar character who weaves and unweaves her tapestries.

So, their encounter has a hidden cosmic symbolism associated with it, and when the sun and the moon come round to coincide once again, Ben Kenobi is simply deleted from existence like an eclipse over the sun. Vader thinks he is victorious and has avenged his defeat at the hands of Kenobi nineteen years earlier. But instead, Kenobi's disappearance— corresponding with a secret and little known cosmic cycle—has transformed him into a ubiquitous presence who is everywhere and nowhere all at once, since he is now coterminous with the field of the Force.

Kenobi, in other words, has become *larger* than Darth Vader: whereas Vader has had to use mechanical technology to make himself into a huge imposing giant of a figure, Kenobi's disappearance into the Force transforms him into a truly *cosmic* figure, as ubiquitous and omnipresent as a god.

Battle with the T.I.E. Fighters
(1:33:16 – 1:38:09)

As the *Millenium Falcon* sails away from the giant mechanical orb, there is a shot of a despondent Luke sitting at the gaming table with Princess Leia and the droids. She maternally places a blanket over him while he tells her that he can't believe that Kenobi is gone. Leia reassures him that there wasn't anything he could have done to save him. (As we have seen, Kenobi and Vader were part of a much larger, cosmic agenda that has all the markings of "fate" written upon it).

But the Empire's sentry ships, meanwhile, are catching up to them: four or five T.I.E. fighters are roaring into outer space just behind them, and Solo comes out to the lounge area to tell Luke that they aren't out of the woods yet. Solo goes *up* a ladder leading to an upper gun bay, while Luke goes *down* the same ladder leading to another gun bay. (These directional vectors point interestingly ahead at the respective directions of the two protagonists in *The Empire Strikes Back*, in which Luke proceeds *downward* on a journey to the Underworld of Dagobah, and Solo, together with Princess Leia, travels *upward* to the realm of the Spirit and to the mechanized Cloud City).

The two protagonists, wired into their gun bays, then begin a shoot-out with the T.I.E. fighters, which come spinning and angling at them firing electrifying bolts of green, while Luke and Han Solo retaliate with blasts of red laser bolts from the ship's guns. Each man has a little video monitor in front of him upon which there is a grid depicting the incoming T.I.E. fighters as tiny little triangles. After a few minutes of shooting, the two are successful at destroying all the ships.

However, in a scene that takes place back on the Death Star, Tarkin and Vader are shown standing side by side. Tarkin asks Vader if he's sure the homing beacon that has been planted onboard the *Falcon* is secure, because he is taking a huge risk letting them go. He hopes that it works.

Solo, meanwhile, returns to the pilot's seat, where Princess Leia is sitting beside him. He congratulates himself on the rescue, but Leia is smart: she knows the Empire has let them get away and is tracking them, although Solo scoffs at such an idea. Leia says that she hopes that when the technical plans of the space station are analyzed a weakness can be found, and says that "we" are not out of this yet. However, Solo—once again as his name implies—does not yet realize that he is part of a tetramorphic protagonist who has become inseparably welded together with the other three. He insists that he isn't interested in any revolution but only wants to be well paid—he has, after all, to think of the "prison" that he alone, now, of all the characters remains stuck inside of regarding his debt to Jabba—and she tells him that if money is all he wants, money is all he'll get.

She leaves the cockpit and tells Luke, who is on his way in, that she wonders if Solo cares about anything other than himself. Luke tells her, *he* does, but she does not appear to hear him.

Luke seats himself in the cockpit beside Solo and asks him what his opinion of the girl is. Solo feigns indifference, to which Luke replies, "Good." Then, noticing Luke's erotic interest in her, he teases him and asks him if could imagine a guy like himself with a princess, to which Luke replies with a firm "No."

There follows an exterior shot of the *Falcon* headed toward a huge red planet, behind which there is a blue-green moon that looks suspiciously like earth.

The sequence with the shooting down of the T.I.E. Fighters using video-game like monitors would appear to be the origins of the arcade video games that soon exploded out of Japan and America only a year or two later after the film's release. The tiny ships represented as triangles on the red video screens resemble the triangular ships of the arcade game called *Asteroids* (1979). *Space Invaders* (1978) and *Galaxia,* moreover, came out at just about the same time. Eventually these games led to the Atari home gaming systems of the 1980s and then to the eventual cinematic feel of today's games like *Call of Duty* and *Grand Theft Auto,* the graphics of which are almost indistinguishable in many cases from the CGI graphics used in today's digital movies. And the training of today's drone pilots very often uses simulators with similar graphics and video game-playing enthusiasts as their pilots.[46]

So this apparently innocuous scene in *Star Wars* had a hugely influential and asymmetric effect on Western culture, leading eventually to the successful capturing of the earth inside the roving flying eyes of drones that look for escaped signifiers or anything that could form a potential military target.

The Empire in *Star Wars* was *not* defeated, which is why more *Star Wars* films are on the way, for the conflict between the local and the global is not only ongoing, but it has heated up into a new global Hot War of jihadists vs. video game tacticians.

Preparing for the Attack

(1:38:10 – 1:45:04)

The *Millenium Falcon* is then shown flying into the airspace of one of the moons of the red planet Yavin. The moon is a jungle planet infested with dense green vegetation and the stony, cracked ruins of old temples left behind by some long-forgotten civilization. Inside one of the temples, the interior space has been transformed into a hangar for the collection of a battle fleet of X-Wing and Y-Wing fighter planes. Solo, Leia and Luke are in the process of being transported on a cart to the commander, who greets Princess Leia and tells her he is glad she is alive. She tells him that the technical read-outs for the Death Star are inside the R2 unit and constitute their only hope.

In the next scene, R2D2 is being plugged into a computer system with a screen that then plays back the data of a three-dimensional read-out of the Death Star. It is a yellow, computerized orb that turns round X-ray style to reveal its inner components.

Meanwhile, the real Death Star—an enormous and solemn gray-white entity--is shown sailing through space on its way to the red planet of Yavin, having been tied to the *Falcon* by the umbilical cord of the homing beacon that was planted there. A shot from inside the conference room of the

Death Star shows Vader and Tarkin receiving word that the planet Yavin has come into view and that the location of the rebel base on a small moon on the other side of the planet has been found. They are preparing to enter the red planet's orbital trajectory.

In a meeting room inside the rebel base, meanwhile, the Commander of the rebellion is shown giving a briefing to an audience of fighter pilots suited up in orange jump suits who listen to his description of the stations' weakness. He tells them that the station was designed to repel large scale attacks, but not an attack from a small one-man fighter. He goes on to say that the approach to the Death Star will not be easy, and that they must fly through a narrow trench leading to a small thermal exhaust port that is only two meters wide and requires a pilot to hit it directly in order to set off a chain reaction inside the Death Star that will blow it up. There is considerable consternation in the room when the pilots realize what they're in for, and one of them, sitting beside Luke, says that a target that small is impossible for a one-man fighter to hit. But Luke tells him he used to bull's eye womp rats on his home planet and that they are not much bigger than two meters. The commander then wraps up the briefing, tells them to man their ships and wishes that the Force be with them.

There follows a shot inside the Death Star upon which a large video monitor screen shows the red planet of Yavin transparent to the small green moon behind it. An impersonal voice comes over the intercom and informs them that the moon with the rebel base upon it will be in firing range in approximately 30 minutes. Vader, standing beside Tarkin, assures him that this will be a day long remembered in history, for it has seen the end of Kenobi, his old nemesis, and will also see the final end of the rebellion. Tarkin, standing to Vader's right side, however, looks nervous.

In the next scene, Luke approaches Han Solo wearing his orange pilot's jump suit and carrying a dingy white helmet, while Solo and Chewbacca are loading up manila-colored boxes full of reward money. Luke tells him that he is disappointed to find Han leaving, but Solo tells him in reply that fighting that battle station isn't his idea of courage but something more akin to suicide. Luke tells him to look after himself with a certain degree of bitterness, and then adds, "I guess that's what you're best at," before walking away. Solo stops him and wishes that the Force will be with him.

As the X-wings are being prepared for combat with R2 units being loaded into each one, Princess Leia notices Luke and asks him why he is despondent, and Luke replies that he is disappointed that Han has chosen to leave them. But Leia tells Luke that Han must follow his own path, kisses him, and then walks away.

There follows a brief scene in the 1997 version of the film that has been added back in, in which an old friend of Luke's named Biggs from the planet of Tatooine greets him with recognition and surprise. (This scene forms the symmetrical conclusion to a never restored scene that was shot on Tatooine at a place called Tosche Station, in which Luke and Biggs are shown talking to each other about the rebellion and Luke maintaining that he cannot join it because of his duties as a farmer. But the scene is awkwardly directed and slow-paced, so it was ultimately never restored).

Then, as Luke climbs up the ladder to his X-Wing fighter craft, the men atop it who are already installing R2D2 note that the droid is a bit beat up and ask Luke if he wants a newer one. Luke tells them no way, as he and the droid have been through too much together to be separated now.

Then as Luke climbs into his craft and straps in, his

plane begins to lift off, and he hears the voice of Ben Kenobi in his head again, telling him not to worry, that the Force will be with him.

There follows a shot of a fleet of X-Wings lifting off and racing out above the dense jungle canopy, with the giant red planet of Yavin in the sky painted over with mother-of-pearl colored clouds.

Now, the cosmology of the ancients was based upon the idea that the earth was at the center of the solar system, and that the sun, together with the other planets, the moon, Mercury, Venus, Mars, Jupiter and Saturn revolved around it as tiny spheres of dense, localized matter that were in turn embedded within huge, invisible etheric spheres that revolved around the earth, one within the other, each revolution of each orb making the sound of one note of the diatonic musical scale. The earth, clear up to about the sixteenth century, was encased, then, on the *inside* of a protective exoskeleton made out of etheric orbs that functioned as a kind of cosmic immune system.

When Copernicus, in the middle of the sixteenth century had his treatise *On the Revolutions of the Celestial Spheres* published (after his death), he decentered the entire model by reviving the ancient heliocentric model of Aristarchus and situating all the planets around the sun. This marked the beginnings of the end of the old model, although Copernicus didn't think he was inaugurating any sort of astronomical revolution, for he was trying to go *back* to Plato's idea that the planets move in perfect circles, and he thought that the only way he could restore the perfect circularity of their motion was to retrieve the heliocentric cosmology with which to do so. His "revolution," then was entirely accidental.

But soon, with Galileo's telescope and Kepler's laws of

planetary motion, it was realized that not only was Copernicus right and the ancients wrong, but that the planets did not move as perfect circles but rather in ellipses with varying speeds and varying motions. By the seventeenth century the ancient exoskeleton surrounding the earth was gone, and it lay unprotected to impacts from the heavens—and from the spirit world—from then on.

The Death Star, on the other hand, is a mechanical orb that attempts to replace those ancient etheric spheres protecting the earth with a mechanized exoskeleton composed of hi-tech satellites in orbit around it in the exosphere, and drones roving through the stratosphere. To the invisible ether of which the ancient spheres were made, there now corresponds the invisible electromagnetic spectrum that ensheaths the planet in a cocoon of pulse signals, so that the entire planet now exists on the *inside* of a technological orb.

The Death Star is simply a metaphor for this techno-orb. It is designed to encase the earth in an exoskeleton of technology that will replace the more elegant etheric technology of the ancient cosmology of spheres within spheres.

But the rebellion, as it prepares to leave the jungle planet behind--which is another metaphor for the earth--in order to crack and disintegrate the Death Star from within, has not, it seems, thought about what they would replace the exoskeleton of the Death Star surrounding and encasing the earth with. Once the Death Star is destroyed, i.e. once the earth is liberated from this false exoskeleton made out of hi-technologies such as satellites and GPS coordinates, the earth will revert back to its state of *throwness* out into the cosmos, unprotected by any immune system, either technological or etheric, other than its atmosphere.[47]

And the death of this "death star" exoskeleton will also

leave behind it the residue that it has generated from the burning of fossil fuels in the form of a dome of greenhouse gases that are currently melting its polar ice caps and causing its sea levels to rise. Soon, our coastal cities will be inundated with floods from tsunamis, storm surges and rising water levels that they will have to erect barriers against.

So, the destruction of the Death Star would, metaphorically speaking, dismantle the earth's outer tropospheric, stratospheric and exospheric layers of technical enframing, but it remains unclear what the rebels think the protective dome would be replaced by.

Today, as Peter Sloterdijk has pointed out in his *Spheres* trilogy, it is all a matter of orbs: who or what is contained inside of what, and where.

The Attack on the Death Star

(1:45:05 – 1:57:46)

In a beautifully retouched CGI scene for the 1997 edition of the film, an army of X-Wings is shown flying in formation past the red planet of Yavin and rounding it as the Death Star comes into view on the other side. At the time of their launch, they had fifteen minutes to travel around Yavin to get to the Death Star. Princess Leia is shown looking down at a map that neatly recapitulates our theory of the battle of spheres that is involved in this climactic sequence, for the round electronic table that she stands beside to observe the fight shows not the ships but a single large round red disc represesnting Yavin, while to the right of this is a smaller blue disc representing the moon upon which the rebel base is located. On the other side of the red Yavin disc is an orange disc with an X drawn across it that represents the Death Star slowly coming into range of the moon. The map is almost an electronified version of those old maps of the ancients depicting the cosmology of spheres within spheres.

But what the map makes clear in this sequence is that *Star Wars* is a film about a battle between orbs: first, the escape from the orb of Tatooine; then the escape from the artificial orb of the Death Star; and now the final climactic battle of the blue-green orb of Yavin's moon against the gray metallic menace of the deadly space station. Should the space station happen to come into range of the moon before the rebels destroy it, it would destroy yet another world just as we have already seen it destroy Alderaan. In other words, the global Anti-World erases and effaces another local cultural horizon from the maps, dissolving it into the homogenous GPS grid of value-neutral coordinates that it has swallowed the whole planet inside.

But if the rebels destroy the artificial orb of the Death Star before it comes into range of the moon, then the entire Global Positioning System surrounding the planet earth disappears and all the lights go out (as it were). If the rebels win, it is a victory of the local, the specific and the ethnic against the universally homogenized Anti-World of Non-Places which the Empire symbolizes in the film.

Currently, the attack proceeds as the X-Wings spread their wings into X-shaped attack patterns and then dive down to the space station's surface to begin their various attempts at flying along its artificial equator made out of a trench of angular structures lined with defensive howitzers and anti-aircraft guns. One by one—and there are only 30 rebel ships—the ships of the rebellion are shot down by howitzers and then by a wave of T.I.E. fighters which comes in on their tails, chasing them along the trench.

Darth Vader decides to climb inside his own ship to fight the rebels, escorted on both sides by traditional T.I.E. fighters. He plows through one rebel ship after the other, until he gets to Luke's X-Wing, upon which he remarks to himself that the Force is particularly strong with this one.

All of Luke's escorts have been blown to pieces by the time he makes it to the central run down the trench. He hears the voice of Ben advising him to turn off his navi-computer and to only use the Force, or, in other words, to just rely on his instincts for the final parting shot.

146

Vader is just about to shoot him down, however, when Han Solo's *Millenium Falcon* shows up at the last minute and shoots down his escorts, knocking Vader's ship out of control and sending him spiraling, momentarily anyway, off into space.

Solo, in the film's climactic moment, tells Luke to blow up the Death Star and finish this thing off, and Luke immediately fires two proton torpedoes into the two meter trench that are a direct hit.

A wide angle shot then shows the few remaining ships of the rebellion quickly fleeing the Death Star just as it has come into range of Yavin's moon and is preparing to blow it to pieces. The Death Star then explodes as Luke's torpedoes hit their target.

A shot of Vader righting his ship and orienting himself then follows.

Meanwhile, the *Millenium Falcon*, together with the rest of the ships of the rebellion fly back to the moon on the other side of Yavin.

It has been a battle of spheres against spheres, this film: first, the escape from the planet of Tatooine occupied the film's first half, for Tatooine is a waste land planet of prisons in which anyone misfortunate enough to find themselves located there is usually stuck, caught or captured somehow in one sort of entanglement or another. Tatooine is the place of entanglements; it is the home of the God Who Binds.

The orb of the Death Star, on the other hand, is simply one giant prison: it is designed to be the Orb of All Orbs, a mechanical planet that is capable of destroying all other planets simply by engulfing them and swallowing them up. It is Heidegger's entire philosophy of the enframing effects of technology visualized as a single orb that wishes to swallow up inside of it every other orb, as though it were a dragon—like the Chinese dragon with the pearl of the sun in its mouth—bent on consuming every planet that it encountered.

The moon of Yavin upon which the rebel base is located—the film's third sphere, although Alderaan functioned briefly as a fourth until it was blown up—is simply the earth at its tropical jungle latitudes located along the equator south of its desert zones to the north (which Tatooine had signified). It is not a waste land image, but a place that is squirming with ancient cellular and zoological life. It is a planet of animals and trees and ecosystems that is pitted in polar opposition to the cold metallic wastes of the Death Star, an artificial planet that is utterly barren of all ecosystems and carries only human lives who have been deworlded from other worlds. The Death Star is an Anti-World, a global ecumene in *Vorhandenheit* mode, going along deworlding other worlds and entities as it travels through space.

Its destruction, however, by Luke Skywalker is only a temporary node of the Empire, which is ruled by an Emperor whom we have not met in the present film. Out of all six films thus far, however, *Star Wars* is really the only film that pits spheres against spheres, a literal war of orbs against one another fighting for domination of two different ways of life: one based on submission to vast, impersonal bureaucratic systems of control and manipulation that have the effect of de-worlding all entities; or one based upon the embeddedness of entities within worlds and ecosystems as webs making such worlds possible in the first place.

The Ceremony
(1:57:47 – 2:00:13)

Luke is shown climbing up out of his X-Wing, once it has returned to the rebel fortress, to the applause of the other rebels. Princess Leia hugs him when he climbs out. R2, however, has suffered a worse fate, and as they pull him out of the craft, he looks completely demolished. C3P0 hopes that they can repair him and adds that he will gladly donate any circuits or parts necessary for the job, but they assure him that R2 will be fine.

A brief shot, then, follows of Princess Leia walking between Han and Luke, all three locked together, shoulder to shoulder.

The film's final shot takes place in the interior of one of the ruined temples that has been cleared out for a huge award ceremony. Han, Luke and Chewbacca enter the hallway, which is guarded by a pair of guards to either side, and they stride down the central corridor in a room that is filled with hundreds of people, all aligned carefully in rows.

They stop before the steps upon which Princess Leia, with a silver necklace and a different hair-do, awaits them with a newly polished C3P0 and R2D2 gleaming behind her. The Commander of the rebellion then hands her a pair of gold medals. She places the first around Han's neck, who winks at her in response, then places the second around

Luke's neck, who is wearing a yellow jacket. Then they all turn and face the crowd to cheers and applause and the film fades out while the final credits roll.

Thus, the War of the Spheres has ended with the transformation and sublimation of the spheres into two gold discs that Princess Leia awards to the two solar heroes who have saved the day. The tetramorphic Subject of Han, Luke, Leia and Chewbacca all stand gathered together on the steps as a single unified Individual, with the two droids behind them functioning as supplements to the tetramorph. The golden exoskeleton of C3P0, and the shiny silver revolving head of R2D2 gleam like the final products of an alchemical operation that has produced the highest, most sublimated metals in the form of silver and gold. But it is gold that predominates in this scene, for it is gold that has been produced out of the union of the pairs of opposites of Han and Luke, Leia and Chewbacca that diagram the tetramorphic Subject which the narrative has produced.

It is a fourfold Subject, moreover, which forms a mandala that is capable of uniting and integrating all worldly spheres.

Appendix:
On the Elements of *Star Wars*

AXIOM 1. All circles, curves and curvilinear trajectories are female; they are therefore "uteromorphic" in nature.

Corollary. The mother produces and generates biological beings.

AXIOM 2. All angles—whether obtuse, right-angled, scalene, etc—including straight lines, are masculine.

Corollary 1. The father produces, from out of his paternal womb, weapons, walls, cities and projectiles of any, and every, sort. Athena, born from the skull of Zeus, and armed with a spear, is essentially a weapon produced from the paternal womb.

Corollary 2. The father hunts down biological beings with angular weapons, and using various arcs, trajectories and angles, destroys them either for food, or to win in battle.

PROPOSITION 1. The zodiac is circular and is therefore a uteromorphic structure.

Postulate. The zodiac is composed of 12 signs.

PROPOSITION 2. The angles formed by the planets, e.g. right angles, squares, oppositions, etc. are masculine and are contained on the *inside* of the zodiac, which functions as a uteromorphic container within which they are inscribed. They are on the *inside* of the mother's body. But with the surrounding of the earth by satellites, this order was reversed and the round sphere of the earth was encompassed and surrounded by the masculine technologies born through the paternal womb of the Metaphysical Age (think here, not only of Athena, but of the Christ-being, incarnate as the Logos, uttered as the Word from the Father's mouth [the Metaphysical Age begins not with Plato, as Heidegger insisted, but rather with Moses and Homer]).

PROPOSITION 3. In the ancient art of divination known as astrology, there are twelve houses in addition to twelve signs of the zodiac. Though the zodiac and the planets will not concern us here, the outer shell of the surrounding "Houses" are of very great value for illuminating the signifiers of *Star Wars*.

Postulate 1. The Tenth House, for instance, is known as the House of the Father.

Postulate 2. Its opposite house, namely, the Fourth House, is known as the House of the Mother.

Postulate 3. The Sixth House is called the House of Small Animals.

Definition. "Small animals," as in learning to manage difficult tasks and / or mastering a discipline.

Postulate 4. The opposing house to the Sixth is the Twelfth. It is known as the House of Large Animals.

Definition. "Large Animals," as in Zodiacal Animals, archetypes of the collective unconscious and / or institutions. Entities, in other words, that require the attainment of the skills and mastery of the Sixth House in order to confront them.

PROPOSITION 4. The city did not become truly "uteromorphic" until it attained the status of a modern sphere. A sphere is a uterine container. The cities of the ancient world, despite the insistences of Lewis Mumford and Peter Sloterdijk to the contrary, were not truly uteromorphic, since they were not actually coterminous with the globe of the earth itself. An ancient city or polis surrounded by a wall is actually *exoskeletal* in nature rather than uteromorphic, strictly speaking. (They rarely occur in the form of perfect circles, although ancient cities like Mari and Baghdad were circular in shape). Most ancient cities had protective outer shells in the form of walls encasing the soft pink anatomies inside them.

Corollary. Those characters in *Star Wars* who can be termed "exoskeletal," i.e. wear outer shells to encase their inner anatomies, are always given a negative valency (i.e. they are on the Dark Side). They are like the early prehistoric fish known as Placoderms, which at first had bony outer shells that gradually vanished over time in favor of the speed and mobility given to them without the shell casings. Characters, then, such as Darth Vader, Boba Fett or the stormtroopers are "Placodermic" in nature. Those characters opposing them never wear bony outer shells. They are exposed and vulnerable, and they signify a "mammalian" evolutionary advance over the Placoderms and reptiles (for instance, stormtroopers riding on giant lizards, etc.).

PROPOSITION 5. The First House is known as the House of the Self.

PROPOSITION 6. Its opposing house, the Seventh, is known as the House of Partners; partners, that is, who are on an equal footing, whether of a romantic or bellicose nature. In order to attain to the Seventh House, wherein one may confront one's enemies on an equal footing, one must first have mastered the Small Animals of the Sixth House.

PROPOSITION 7. The attainment of the Self in the First House is known as "Individuation," and leads to the acquisition of one's personal belongings in the Second House. One can then stand up to the Large Animals of the

Twelfth House (after having mastered the difficult tasks of the Sixth House, that is).

CONCLUSION. Thus, though the exoskeleton of astrology can be used as a tool to shed considerable light upon the semiotics of *Star Wars*, the actual "material" of astrology, i.e. planets and their transits, are of no use to us and will be discarded for this reading.

Endnotes

Introduction: On *Star Wars* as the American National Epic

1. Joel Garreau, *The Nine Nations of North America* (New York: Avon Books, 1982).

2. Marshall McLuhan, *Understanding Media* (Boston: MIT Press, 1994).

3. See, for instance, Marshall McLuhan, *Culture is Our Business* (New York: McGraw Hill, 1970).

4. Lucas originally wanted to make Flash Gordon into a movie, but couldn't get the rights. Luke Skywalker, then, is the blonde solar hero equivalent to Flash Gordon, and he comes up out of the underworld of his pit house on Tatooine like the sun emerging from the Underworld in ancient Egyptian cosmology.

5. Darth Vader is simply a reterritorialized Dr. Doom.

6. Roland Barthes, *Mythologies* (New York: Hill and Wang, 1972).

7. See, in particular, Jean Baudrillard, *The System of Objects* (London: Verso Books, 1996; orig. pub. 1968).

8. Peter Sloterdijk, *In the World Interior of Capital: For a Philosophical Theory of Globalization* (United Kingdom: Polity Books, 2013), 167ff.

The Opening Crawl: "Episode 4: A New Hope"

9. In the original 1977 theatrical release, the title "Episode IV: A New Hope" was absent, and the crawl came forward before the title "*Star Wars*" had completely receded into deep space. The film's subtitle was added only after the re-release of the film in 1981 after *The Empire Strikes Back* had been released in 1980.

10. James Joyce, *Finnegans Wake* (New York: Penguin Books, 1976), 598.

11. The term "uteromorphic" comes from Peter Sloterdijk, *Spheres I: Bubbles* (Los Angeles: Semiotexte, 2011), 279.

The Capture of Princess Leia

12. *Abgrund*, or *der Abgrund*, to be more precise, is the German word for "abyss," and it is a term frequently used by Heidegger in his writings to connote the bottomless abyss from out of which being comes.

13. For the concept of *Vorhandenheit*, see Martin Heidegger, *Being and Time* (New York: Harper-Perennial, 1962), 48. For the concept of "worldlessness," however, see 81-82.

14. Mumford's conception of the history of technology as having three phases, Eotechnic, Paleotechnic and Neotechnic may be found in Lewis Mumford, *Technics and Civilization* (New York: Harcourt Brace, 1963), 107ff.

15. The concept of "codes," "overcoding," and "coding the flows" comes from Gilles Deleuze and Felix Guattari, *Anti-Oedipus: Capitalism and Schizophrenia* (New York: Penguin Books, 1977), 36ff.

16. For an excellent discussion of the 12 Houses of

Astrology, see the following YouTube video in which Arthur Young explains them: https://www.youtube.com/watch?v=UVl8pGGimCk

The Capture of the Droids

17. The best explanation of this myth may be found in Hans Jonas, *The Gnostic Religion* (Boston: Beacon Press, 2001).

Introduction of Luke Skywalker

18. For the best introduction to the work of Ray Harryhausen, the reader should consult Ray Harryhausen, *Film Fantasy Scrapbook* (UK: Gazelle Book Services Ltd, 1975).

19. Michael Hardt and Antonio Negri, *Empire* (Harvard University Press, 2001).

The Discovery of the Message

20. For this myth, see Geo Widengren, *Mani and Manichaeism* (New York: Holt, Rinehart and Winston, 1965).

The Escape of R2D2

21. See the entry "Dromoscopy" by John David Ebert in John Armitage, ed., *The Virilio Dictionary* (Edinburgh University Press, 2013).

22. For the concept of "throwness" in Heidegger see "Falling and Throwness" in Martin Heidegger, *Being and Time*, ibid., 219ff.

23. James Howard Kunstler, *The Geography of Nowhere* (New York: Touchstone, 1993).

24. Marc Auge, *Non-Places: An Introduction to Supermodernity* (UK: Verso Books, 2009).

Introduction of Ben Kenobi

25. Jean Gebser, *The Ever-Present Origin* (Ohio University Press, 1985), 45ff.

Introduction of the Death Star

26. The concept of "Universal States" comes from Arnold Toynbee, *A Study of History* (New York: Weathervane Books, 1972), 255ff.

27. For the concept of things "thinging," see the essay "The Thing" in Martin Heidegger, *Poetry, Language, Thought* (NY: Harper Perennial, 2001), 163ff.

28. For the idea of *Ereignis* as an "event," see Martin Heidegger, *Contributions to Philosophy (of the Event)* (Indiana University Press, 2012).

The Deaths of Uncle Own and Aunt Beru

29. This scene may be found in the Blu-Ray edition of *The Searchers* at 21:40.

The Torture of Princess Leia

30. For the concepts of the biopolitical and zoe, or "bare naked life," see Giorgio Agamben, *Homo Sacer: Sovereign Power and Bare Life* (Stanford University Press, 1998). The

idea of "biopolitics" originated however in Michel Foucault, *The History of Sexuality, Volume I: An Introduction* (NY: Vintage Books, 1990), 133ff.

Mos-Eisley Spaceport

31. See the essay entitled "The City in the Age of Touristic Reproduction" in Boris Groys, *Art Power* (Boston: MIT Press, 2008), 101ff.

Introduction of Han Solo

32. For Heidegger's concept of technology as "enframing" the earth, see the essay "The Question Concerning Technology" in Martin Heidegger, *The Question Concerning Technology & Other Essays* (NY: Harper-Perennial, 1977), 3ff.

Jabba the Hut

33. See the essay "*The Maltese Falcon* & the Cosmology of San Francisco," in John David Ebert, *Gods & Heroes of the Media Age: From Captain Nemo to* The X-Files (Eugene, Oregon: Post Egoism Media, 2015), 67ff.

Flight From the Desert Planet

34. The concept of "assemblages" comes from Deleuze & Guattari. See the entry, "Assemblages," in Gilles Deleuze & Felix Guattari, *A Thousand Plateaus: Capitalism and Schizophrenia* (University of Minnesota Press, 1987), 503-505.

35. The idea of the "jump into hyperspace" can be found

in Isaac Asimov, *Foundation* (New York: Bantam Dell, 1979), 4-5.

36. For the eagle that carries Vainamoinen on its back to Pohjola, see "Poem 7" in Elias Lonnrot, ed. *The Kalevala: Or Poems of the Kaleva District* (Harvard University Press, 1963), 37ff.

The Destruction of Alderaan

37. Alain Badiou, *Ethics: an Essay on the Understanding of Evil* (UK: Verso, 2002), 4-17.

38. The concept of the "sign regime" comes from D&G. See the chapter "587 BC – AD 70: On Several Regimes of Signs," in Deleuze and Guattari, *A Thousand Plateaus*, ibid., 111ff.

Luke's First Training Lesson

39. See Immanuel Kant, *Critique of Pure Reason* (NY: St Martin's Press, 1929).

40. A good and accessible alternative to reading *Being and Time* regarding Heidegger's meaning of Dasein is to read instead an early lecture version of *Being and Time*. See Martin Heidegger, *History of the Concept of Time: Prolegomena* (Indiana University Press, 1992), 151-167.

Captured by the Death Star

41. Specifically, it may be found in the Blu-Ray Criterion Edition of *Sanjuro* at 12:45.

42. "Striated space" as opposed to "smooth space" also

comes from D&G and may be found in the chapter entitled "1440: the Smooth and the Striated" in D&G, *A Thousand Plateaus*, ibid., 474ff.

The Rescue of Princess Leia

43. See the chapter entitled "The Dynamo and the Virgin" in Henry Adams, *The Education of Henry Adams* (Blacksburg, VA: Wilder Publications, 2008), 243.

44. See John David Ebert, *The Age of Catastrophe: Disaster and Humanity in Modern Times* (Jefferson, North Carolina: McFarland & Co., 2012).

Trash Compactor

45. The best analysis of the figure of the "midden heap" and its significance may be found in Marhsall McLuhan, *From Cliché to Archetype* (Berkeley, CA: Gingko Press, 2011), 94-100. "The middenhide," he there writes on page 102, "grows mountainous with the castoffs of cultures and technologies."

Battle with the T.I.E. Fighters

46. See my essays, "The Killing Eye: Video Games, Surrogate Violence and the Dismantling of Social Machines" and "Robots, Drones and the Disappearance of the Human Being," in John David Ebert, *The New Media Invasion: Digital Technologies and the World They Unmake* (Jefferson, North Carolina: McFarland & Co., 2011).

Preparing for the Attack

47. See Peter Sloterdijk's discussion of the ontological

consequences of "spherelessness" in the Introduction entitled "The Allies; or the Breathed Commune" to *Spheres Volume I: Bubbles, Microspherology* (Los Angeles, CA: Semiotexte, 2012), 24-25.

Bibliography

Adams, Henry. *The Education of Henry Adams*. Blacksburg, VA: Wilder Publications, 2008.

Agamben, Giorgio. *Homo-Sacer: Sovereign Power and Bare Life*. Stanford University Press, 1998.

Armitage, John, ed. *The Virilio Dictionary*. Edinburgh University Press, 2013.

Asimov, Isaac. *Foundation*. New York: Bantam Dell, 1979.

Auge, Marc. *Non-Places: An Introduction to Supermodernity*. UK: Verso Books, 2009.

Badiou, Alain. *Ethics: an Essay on the Understanding of Evil*. UK: Verso, 2002.

Barthes, Roland. *Mythologies*. New York: Hill and Wang, 1972.

Baudrillard, Jean. *The System of Objects*. London: Verso Books, 1996.

Deleuze, Gilles and Guattari, Felix. *Anti-Oedipus: Capitalism and Schizophrenia*. New York: Penguin Books, 1977.

___, and ___. *A Thousand Plateaus: Capitalism and Schizophrenia*. University of Minnesota Press, 1987.

Ebert, John David. *The Age of Catastrophe: Disaster and Humanity in Modern Times*. Jefferson, North Carolina: McFarland & Co., 2012.

___. *Gods & Heroes of the Media Age: From Captain*

Nemo to The X-Files. Eugene, Oregon: Post Egoism Media, 2015.

___. *The New Media Invasion: Digital Technologies and the World They Unmake*. Jefferson, North Carolina: McFarland & Co., 2011.

Foucault, Michel. *The History of Sexuality, Volume I: An Introduction*. New York: Vintage Books, 1990.

Garreau, Joel. *The Nine Nations of North America*. New York: Avon Books, 2011.

Gebser, Jean. *The Ever-Present Origin*. Ohio University Press, 1985.

Groys, Boris. Art Power. Boston: MIT Press, 2008.

Hardt, Michael and Negri, Antonio. *Empire*. Harvard University Press, 2001.

Harryhausen, Ray. *Film Fantasy Scrapbook*. UK: Gazelle Book Services Ltd., 1975.

Heidegger, Martin. *Being and Time*. New York: HarperPerennial, 1962.

___. *Contributions to Philosophy (of the Event)*. Indiana University Press, 2012.

___. *History of the Concept of Time: Prolegomena*. Indiana University Press, 1992.

___. *Poetry, Language, Thought*. New York: HarperPerennial, 2001.

___. *The Question Concerning Technology & Other Essays*. New York: HarperPerennial, 1977.

Jonas, Hans. *The Gnostic Religion*. Boston: Beacon Press, 2001.

Joyce, James. *Finnegans Wake*. New York: Penguin Books, 1976.

Kant, Immanuel. *Critique of Pure Reason*. New York: St. Martin's Press, 1929.

Lonnrot, Elias, ed. *The Kalevala: Or Poems of the Kaleva*

District. Harvard University Press, 1963.

Kunstler, James Howard. *The Geography of Nowhere*. New York: Touchstone, 1993.

McLuhan, Marshall. *Culture is Our Business*. New York: McGraw Hill, 1970.

___. *From Cliché to Archetype*. Berkeley, CA: Gingko Press, 2011.

___. *Understanding Media*. Boston: MIT Press, 1994.

Mumford, Lewis. *Technics and Civilization*. New York: Harcourt Brace, 1963.

Sloterdijk, Peter. *In the World Interior of Capital: For a Philosophical Theory of Globalization*. UK: Polity Books, 2013.

___. *Spheres I: Bubbles, Microspherology*. Los Angeles: Semiotexte, 2011.

Toynbee, Arnold. *A Study of History*. New York: Weathervane Books, 1972.

Widengren, Geo. *Mani and Manichaeism*. New York: Holt, Rinehart and Winston, 1965.

Made in United States
North Haven, CT
29 December 2022